FÉIDHLIM HARTY

GET RID OF YOUR BIN

And Save Money

MERCIER PRESS
WHAT YOU NEED TO READ

MERCIER PRESS

Cork

www. mercierpress.ie

Trade enquiries to CMD,
55A Spruce Avenue, Stillorgan Industrial Park,
Blackrock, County Dublin

© Féidhlim Harty, 2009

ISBN: 978 1 85635 626 8

10 9 8 7 6 5 4 3 2 1

A CIP record for this title is available from the British Library

Mercier Press receives financial assistance from the Arts Council/An Chomhairle Ealaíon

Mixed Sources
Product group from well-managed forests, and other controlled sources
www.fsc.org Cert no. SGS-COC-1693
© 1996 Forest Stewardship Council

Printed and bound in the EU on FSC approved paper.

CONTENTS

For Susie and Kate

ACKNOWLEDGEMENTS

We are all so reliant upon one another that it is a little sobering. To hint at the huge web that makes up our daily lives just imagine for a moment the sheer number of people involved in the process of providing the basic raw materials to draft this book – even just the pens and paper; from manufacture to use. Needless to say, while writing this book I relied upon them all and wish to acknowledge them gratefully.

There are many others that are more easily identified. José Ospina provided the original excuse to prepare much of the material contained here, while St Brogan's College, the Bandon Family Resource Centre and *Gaelscoil Dhroichead na Banndan* provided the opportunities to host the early 'waste watching' workshops. Once the workshop material reached manuscript stage, the advice and constructive feedback from Pádraig Ó Flaitheartaigh, Treasa Spragg and Natasha Harty was invaluable.

I would like to thank everyone at the Irish Peatland Conservation Council, the Irish Whale and Dolphin Group, ENFO, all the county council environment departments and everyone listed in the appendices for their assistance with specific points of enquiry. Thanks also to Maire Hitching, Doug Phillips, Sinead

McDonnell, Noel Kelly, Declan Gallagher, Isaac and Rachel Allen, Eliz Egan, Piaras Mac Éinrí, Colin Campbell, Ruth McGrath, Tom Roche, Br Anthony and George Whelan for their help along the way. Thank you to Eoin Purcell and all at Mercier Press for their enthusiasm and assistance, and for bringing the idea to the bookshop shelves.

Finally to my wife, editor, business partner and source of support and encouragement, Elinor Hitching: thank you.

INTRODUCTION

➤ Do you want to keep your waste disposal charges to a minimum?

➤ Do you want to minimise your environmental impact?

➤ Did you know that beyond our species, there is no such thing as 'waste' in nature? Surely there is room for improvement on the widespread use of the rubbish bin ...

Armed with some straightforward information and a clear goal in mind, it is quite easy to reduce your rubbish by a surprising amount. With a little vigilance it is possible to bring both your environmental impact and your waste disposal costs down to a minimum.

So to maximise your savings and boost your ecological sustainability, read on and practise from the word go!

Remember – keep the essentials in mind:

Step 1 – **Be ruthless when shopping**. Allow into your home *only* those things that can leave it again without going via the bin.

Step 2 – **Compost** all your kitchen and garden food and plant waste. There are some exceptions depending on your circumstances, but practically everything organic in nature can be composted in one way or another.

Step 3 – **Reuse everything** that you possibly can. Reroute unwanted but functional items to friends, relations, charity shops, bookstores or other places that can find a genuine use for them. Use returnable containers where possible. As a last resort, you can reuse the materials from which your unwanted items are made, by recycling glass, paper, card, plastic, metals and textiles.

Some tools for the journey

Tool 1 – **Information** on composting, waste minimisation, recycling and simplicity is readily available on the internet, in the library, from environmental groups and other sources. Use it to complement this book wherever you come up against a stumbling block and have difficulty getting the volume of your rubbish down to zero.

Tool 2 – **Grow your own** organic vegetables and fruit. Even a 1.2 x 1.2 metre raised bed can keep you in some vegetables all year round and use all the compost you generate. Food from the garden doesn't come in plastic ...

Tool 3 – **Get rid of your bin**. Nothing focuses the mind more than burning your bridges. But do so from a place of informed confidence, not blind ignorance. Read on, make your decision and cancel your bin collection as soon as you are ready.

Our attitude to waste changes over time. A generation or two ago many people would pile up glass and plastic in the garden with their other kitchen compostables as if it would all rot away. Now we wouldn't dream of it, nor do we tolerate dumping rubbish around the countryside. Attitudes do change steadily, however slowly it may seem.

Landfill space is at a premium at present and consequently county councils are putting more efforts into recycling. Legislative requirements are meanwhile pushing both the government and the individual towards waste reduction. Ireland's introduction of a levy on plastic shopping bags is the most obvious sign of this trend, and has effectively removed from our countryside this most unsightly type of wind-blown rubbish. At the same time, steep rises in bin charges have brought waste reduction firmly to the fore in our minds. This reinforces our enthusiasm for saving money in the current economic climate.

In addition to pressures of legislation and cost, as well as the social pressure that we exert on one another, we are also developing a greater awareness of our impact on the wider world. As we learn more about the effects of energy consumption and resource use in manufacturing, we naturally desire to minimise our damage to the world around us. Know-how is the first step; then, as with everything else, regular practice exercises our 'Waste-Not' muscles.

Why should we bother to minimise our waste?

➤ Financial motives

For many, money is the primary consideration. Bin charges have people talking, the media watching and everybody observing their bin weight. Whether you are cash-strapped, thrifty, stingy or just keen not to squander what you have, the financial motive is a significant one.

➤ Environmental reasons

The other obvious motivation is environmental. For over a generation, protection of the environment has been a top priority for those who care about the world around them. Cotton shopping bags were in use by a dedicated minority long before the plastic bag levy. Different people have different environmental concerns, but all (or most anyway) point towards waste reduction. Whether you want to stop an incinerator in your county, tackle litter on your street, protect inland rivers and lakes or the coastline, or tackle local air pollution caused by burning plastic; waste reduction is an active way to minimise your own contribution to the problem you are trying to solve.

➤ Social reasons

Social motivations include legislative pressures, limitations on landfill space and ease of access to recycling depots. People's priorities range broadly. Some people choose to dump illegally, for which public pressure can be an effective motivation to stop. Others have a 'not in my backyard' attitude about littering and landfill sites, in which case making the connection between bin use and landfill requirements can be the catalyst for change. Some have a genuine concern about the world, for which education is essential in encouraging positive change in lifestyle and behaviour.

➤ Health

Health can be linked to both social and environmental motivations. In a direct way, incineration and household burning of plastic contaminate the air we breathe. Landfill leachate can pollute the water we drink, and both air and water contaminants can build up in the food we eat. Happily, waste minimisation and healthy choices often coincide. If we can grow our own salad greens, buy our carrots loose at the local farmers' market and source our eggs from a neighbour who will reuse the boxes, we can both improve our diets and reduce the amount of plastic entering our kitchens.

Head starts

- If you have a garden for composting organic kitchen waste, and for using the compost you make, you have an immediate head start in the waste reduction stakes.
- If you have pets or hens, to eat meat or kitchen scraps

respectively, that is another bonus. Instead of paying to dispose of waste that will eventually rot in landfill, you will be rewarded with the happy companionship of a pet, as well as fresh eggs for breakfast.

- If you have like-minded neighbours who would share your bin, you can halve your standing charges overnight. Talk to the people on your street about sharing resources to cut down on costs.

- If you have a garden shed or shelf space for extra recyclables storage, you have the advantage of being able to do occasional recycling drops to the local bring site instead of paying for collection.

However although the above 'head starts' may be a bonus, it's important to realise that most essential of all is the simple desire to get rid of your bin. A little planning and a lot of imagination can make the whole process as simple and straightforward as you need it to be. Remember: to ensure long-term success, the new set-up needs to be workable day-in, day-out.

How far to go?

Everyone has a different reason for waste reduction and a different degree to which they are prepared to go. If you choose only what is right for you, the chances are that your efforts towards minimisation will be more satisfactory, more entertaining (yes, I consider it a fun challenge!) and ultimately longer lasting.

The first thing to do is to know your priorities. If you are genuinely interested only in your pocket and not in the world around you, your neighbours or even your health, then find out how your bin charges are structured and reduce your weight or volume accordingly (assuming you want to stay within the law, which is indeed to be recommended). If, on the other hand, you are keen to improve your health and contribute positively to the environment, take these considerations into account from the start.

Don't worry about being too consistent in your approach. Recognise that you will be happy to reduce in some areas and not in others. Maybe you will be quite happy to give up the daily paper as a way to reduce your waste, but still like to read novels by the score. That's fine: do what you are comfortable with and be imaginative about your approach. Perhaps the library would provide the novels and you could reduce both sources of paper consumption!

The concept of 'simplicity' is much bandied-about these days as a necessity for stress-free modern living; for the fashionable feng shui house, for example, or for the ultimate in minimalist interior design. However the essence of simplicity is the cultivation of a feeling of 'enough', and a sense of contentment with life and what it offers. This approach doesn't seem to get much media coverage because it doesn't sell advertising space. However, buying less is the ultimate waste minimisation tactic. It also reduces the time you need to spend earning the money both to buy things in the first place, and then to pay for their disposal again. Having studied the different environmentally-friendly building materials on the market for an extension for our cottage, we finally decided on the ultimate environmentally- and financially-friendly approach possible: we did nothing! Overnight the stress of facing another major building project vanished in a puff of logic.

Question: do you want to be rid of your bin? You can, easily. How far you go in that direction is down to you. This book will give you pointers along the way to help reach your destination. Even if you keep up your bin collection, new charging structures make it financially rewarding to minimise your collection frequency and weight. Start now – maximise your ecological sustainability and your savings.

WHY MINIMISE?

There are many compelling reasons for waste minimisation, including:

- Problems associated with disposal
- Impacts on society
- Squandering of resources
- Energy consumption
- Habitat destruction
- Air pollution

Although these categories are listed separately, they are each inextricably linked to one another.

Disposal problems

Dumping waste by legal or illegal methods of disposal has numerous drawbacks. Landfill space is running out in Ireland and new dumps are unpopular with neighbours. Incineration of municipal waste poses a major health hazard, not to mention the additional dangers associated with incineration of toxic wastes. Incineration as a disposal option also eliminates county councils' need for waste minimisation: after all, incinerators need to be fed! Costs of waste disposal are rising by the year, for the government, local councils, industry and homeowners.

Landfill leachate – the liquid that drains from rubbish sent to landfill – is highly polluting when it escapes into groundwater, rivers or streams, and often contains toxic elements. Over the years, solvents, chemicals, batteries and other toxics have made their way into landfill sites and are still contributing to the leachate that emerges. Land contaminated with some wastes can be unusable for generations. Water pollution by leachate, dumping and littering, can be very serious for the aquatic life in streams, rivers and the sea, while even simple plastic six-pack holders can kill fish and sea birds that get tangled up in them.

Even on the domestic scale, inappropriate disposal methods can be detrimental to the environment. Garbage grinders, for example, can increase the level of waste leaving a house by a considerable amount, due to the conversion of compostable materials into additional pollution loads in the sewers. Meanwhile burning of plastics in the fireplace is even more polluting than doing so in incinerators.

Respect for our society

Social responsibilities are being increasingly recognised with regard to waste disposal. Whether we affect our neighbours across the fence, or our neighbouring countries and continents, waste disposal has a complete disregard for boundaries.

Recycling processes have the potential to be quite toxic. Waste electronic equipment and other 'recyclables' are often exported to less affluent countries with lower wages and less stringent environmental, health and safety legislation. Even recyclables such as paper and plastic have the potential to be damaging to health and local environments depending on the processes involved in their recycling.

Transboundary air pollution causes acid rain, ozone depletion and global climate change. What we burn and dispose of into the air in Ireland, whether in our hearths, incinerators or industrial processes, affects not only ourselves and our northern European neighbours, but the whole planet.

Addiction to consumerism is as damaging to individuals and families as many drugs. With our addiction to buying 'stuff' (which we then have to dump, remember?) we have bought ourselves into a hole of debt. It is not uncommon now to see reports of national spending that exceed national earnings! If that isn't addictive behaviour, what is?

Maintaining a stable supply of oil for our endless consumption of plastic products, use of agricultural chemicals and single-occupancy vehicles seems just a little unethical. Oil wars were already being fought in the 1990s and show no signs of abating. Maybe if we all buy a lot less, and slow down a little, oil will begin to lose its hold on our society. With many analysts regarding 'peak oil' – the point at which oil supply is outstripped by demand – as having already been reached, alternative ways of living may be on the horizon.

Water wars are another real possibility. Industrial and agricultural processes can consume vast quantities of water, often in areas that can least afford to squander it. When much of the resulting produce is for export to Europe and the US, it brings home the importance of minimising our buying as well as our waste.

Resource conservation

Waste and resource use are inextricably linked. Fossil fuels have a limited availability: new supplies of coal, oil and gas are diminishing at a shocking rate, and still we use them as if there were no tomorrow. Those who study peak oil suggest that we have reached that point already, hence the rise in oil prices since 2000. There are still reserves of less accessible oil, such as tar sands, but these too are finite, and much more costly and environmentally damaging to extract and process to a usable state. Surely such a resource waste is not only avoidable, but unjustifiable. Yet the waste continues every day in the form of the numerous oil-derived products and services we buy and transport around the globe.

Raw materials such as stone and metals have less serious implications, although they too are being consumed in vast quantities and use enormous amounts of oil and electricity in their processing. Even recycling glass and metals uses energy that is far in excess of sustainable amounts.

Water is an often under-appreciated resource and clean water is much more limited than the rainfall rates in Ireland would have us believe. Excessive wastage or pollution of this resource leads to shortages, even in this country. Climate change is also accentuating the extremes of weather conditions, making dry areas even drier. Wasteful lifestyles have led to these changes, but we can probably still reverse climatic trends with immediate concerted action.

Timber as a resource is replaceable, but not on the scale that we expect it to be available to us for our new oak or mahogany sideboards whenever kitchen fashions change; for toilet paper and tissues; for single-sided, single-use, chlorine-bleached office paper and so on. I am not suggesting we do without loo paper, just that we use a somewhat more appropriate source of fibre than trees. Examples of alternative fibres include recycled paper, hemp, sugar cane, cotton and bamboo. From a waste perspective using recycled paper, or other waste fibre, as your source material keeps that waste out of landfill. Waste and resource use are two sides of the one coin, and we are overspending on a grand scale.

Energy saving
The social, political and environmental impact of energy consumption is clearer now than ever before. Oil wars appear to be a current by-product of the oil industry. Whether it is arrests in Mayo, murder in Nigeria or bombing of the Middle East and Afghanistan, oil in these decades is a cause of conflict. The most effective way to prevent this is to endeavour to eliminate our support for

the industry that carries out the battles in our name. It is almost impossible to avoid oil use at present. This is because it is widely used in conventional agriculture, plastics production, manufacturing, synthetic fibres, cosmetics and cleaning chemicals, transport and travel. However, limiting our energy use and our consumption of products is essential in this context. With a little information and some perseverance in changing our purchasing habits, huge reductions in oil dependency are possible.

Apart from the social strife they cause, the fossil fuels that are used to generate our energy are a limited resource. Wars aside, the issue of peak oil appears to be driving prices up exponentially. Even if the peak oil experts are wrong and prices do fall into the future, it seems inevitable that they will climb again. At some point oil will simply become too scarce to extract economically, or at least in the quantities we are used to.

Global climate change is mainly the result of increasing atmospheric carbon dioxide from burning fossil fuels such as coal, oil and gas. This carbon dioxide acts as an insulating blanket around the planet, allowing in the sun's energy, but preventing it radiating out into space again. As well as a general global increase in temperatures there has been a shift towards greater extremes of climatic conditions. Globally, recent decades have seen some of the hottest summers, mildest winters, longest droughts and most severe floods in recorded history. The shape of our future climate is unknown. If some predictions are correct, Irish temperatures would plummet if the Gulf Stream were to stop bringing warmth to our shores.

In Ireland, our peat bogs have provided us with a fossil fuel source down through the centuries. Unfortunately this resource has experienced an accelerated decline with the advent of mechanical extraction. Burning peat contributes to climate change, as well as destroying the peatland habitat that could otherwise act as a living carbon sink, helping to counter climate change. Irish raised bogs, blanket bogs and fens are home to a rare and diverse range of flora and fauna that need protection if they are to escape extinction. Because peat is limited, whether we halt extraction now or upon reaching full depletion of the resource, it will not affect the economy all that much, but will make a large and lasting difference to the flora and fauna that the habitat supports. Avoiding turf, briquettes and peat moss, and switching to a renewable electricity supplier, such as Airtricity, are very easy steps towards protecting these valuable habitats. Keep an eye out for other renewable suppliers, as this is a sector that is growing all the time.

Clean air

Air pollution from the manufacturing of products, processing of raw materials and production of energy leads to acid rain as well as climate change. Transport of raw materials, products and wastes consumes fossil fuels and produces sulphur dioxide (SO_2), carbon dioxide (CO_2) and other pollutants. Some production processes and products use harmful chemicals. For example CFCs lead to ozone depletion and the associated problems of skin cancers. These chemicals can be present as coolant gases in fridges and freezers or as propellants in aerosol containers and foams. Many changes in industry practice are improving the situation, but how we deal with our waste fridges and freezers, particularly older models, still has a direct impact on the ozone layer.

Incineration of waste produces dioxins and other toxic elements such as mercury, cadmium and lead, not to mention considerable quantities of contaminated ash, all of which still need to be landfilled. Even landfilling waste has an air pollution dimension; resulting in odours which are unpleasant to be around and gases which can be dangerous for nearby houses.

Habitat protection

Habitat destruction and degradation is yet another reason to minimise our waste and our consumption. Our waste mountain is just the visible tip of our overuse of resources. Forests around the world are being cut at a staggering rate for timber and grazing land, mainly for Western furniture, paper and beef. Oil exploration, extraction and transportation put coastal habitats at tremendous risk and degrade habitats on land where spillages occur. From whaling to over-fishing, peat extraction to mining, the over-exploitation of resources impacts seriously on habitats, flora and fauna.

What we do with our waste can have a very serious

direct impact on the environment. Dioxins are produced during waste incineration wherever chlorine compounds such as PVC are included (which is almost always). Leachate from landfills poses a risk to ground water and surface waters when inadequate containment measures are in place. Dumping poorly treated sewage and industrial effluent to sea has implications for coastal habitats. The seal virus of the past number of decades is thought to be exacerbated by water pollution from contaminants such as PCBs. Similarly air pollution, climate change and ozone depletion are all implicated in the ongoing decline in frog populations worldwide, as well as habitat loss. In Ireland, direct links can be drawn between our most polluted water courses and industrial, agricultural or municipal discharges of wastes via effluent.

Physical pressure is another impact on wildlife. The space required for landfill leads to habitat loss, purely in terms of the development of the existing environment at the chosen site. One example is Slieve Felim in County Limerick, where habitat encroachment was one of the many reasons for halting development of the area as a landfill site. Although not a waste per se, habitat loss by new road building could be seen as a waste of both resources and habitat space. With some care, alternative forms of transportation could easily negate the need for the vast new road projects throughout the country.

All in all, there is a clear case to be made for minimising our waste mountain and inextricably linked resource consumption, through our endless desire for more. In our consumer society there is, inherent even in the name, the idea that consumption is our main objective. Always the answer given on TV, radio, magazines and newspapers is 'buy more; go on more holidays; gather more experiences; buy more; spend more money; buy more'. However, we know having more does not lead to contentment. If 'more' is always the answer, surely somewhere along the way we are asking the wrong questions.

How much is enough?

This is a question which has been pondered over millennia, and is now more relevant than ever. Yet 'enough' is something that we are not particularly good at recognising. The ills associated with over-consumption are as clear as day when you open your eyes to them, yet 'enough' still seems to elude us. How many people in the world are dying from starvation and how many are dying from the diseases of excess? Again these are two sides of the same coin. Only by identifying our own 'enough' can we move comfortably away from the mantra of 'more'.

The good news is that you don't need to change the world, you only need to change yourself, and the world will be changed as a consequence.

Meanwhile you can eliminate your bin charges: the last, most popular and probably least important reason to minimise your waste.

WHAT A WASTE –
THE STUFF WE DUMP

When it comes to waste there are endless statistics: tonnages and percentages; sources and relative volumes; increases with time and more. However the most important statistic to remember is simple:

- *We produce too much waste of all types.* Our recycling rate may be increasing, but so too is the volume of waste we produce, and recycling alone, without minimising consumption, is too energy-intensive a process to be environmentally sustainable.

Waste Generation
Waste generation in Ireland is classified by three principal sources:

- **Municipal waste** includes many easily recouped materials such as compostables, glass, paper, timber, plastic and metals. There are also other less valuable resources and more difficult wastes. These include hazardous wastes such as batteries; liquid wastes such as paints, thinners and waste oil; and mixed wastes, which can include all of the above in an inseparable mess that minimises the scope for reuse, maximises the pollution potential and increases the problems of safe handling of what could, if properly sorted, be a valuable resource.

- **Industrial waste** in Ireland is generated primarily in the construction, manufacturing and mining and quarrying industries. Hazardous waste accounts for less than 1 percent of total waste, but constitutes a very difficult waste to deal with sustainably.

  Proper storage and sorting maximises the potential for sale of industrial wastes as resources for other processes. Minimisation not only reduces waste, but makes sound financial sense for the companies that carry it out.

- **Agricultural waste** accounts for the largest volume of waste in Ireland, but includes slurry and farmyard manure and as such is a somewhat misleading term, since these have traditionally been spread on the land to add nutrients. Other wastes involved in agriculture include plastic silage wraps and covers as well as containers from biocide and fertiliser use, which need careful disposal or recycling.

Waste management – where does it go at present?

The very term 'waste' hampers our appreciation of potentially valuable resources. At government level, the hierarchy of *Reduce, Reuse, Recycle* is officially espoused. This proposes that we should first *reduce* the amount of waste we generate, then *reuse* as much as possible and finally *recycle* what is left over. The policy is excellent, but is more difficult to put into practice than to put into print. Constructive steps are being taken at government and county council level to introduce recycling, but recycling alone is insufficient. To verify the popularity of reuse, witness the growth of second-hand shops, charity shops, Buy and Sell, classified supplements and eBay over the past decade or two. Nonetheless, our consumption habits are trying to trip us up with great enthusiasm: our efforts at reduction are in dramatic reverse.

Here is what we currently do with the considerable volume of waste we produce each year:

- Landfill
- Incinerate
- Recycle
- Reuse
- Dump in various ways

➤ Landfill

Landfill is the most popular current method of managing our waste mountain. However, there are a number of problems associated with landfilling waste. The liquid runoff, or leachate, is very polluting and toxic. It contains a diverse range of pollutants generated by any number of wastes in the landfill site. Rotting food provides most of the odour and a lot of the organic pollution load. This is accompanied by waste from batteries, solvents, paints, cosmetics, cleaners and so on. Unless landfill sites are fully lined, leachate can cause serious pollution to local groundwater, streams and rivers. Even when sites are lined, the leachate needs to be removed for treatment. Because of the nature of the waste, full treatment is impossible since many toxic elements can remain in the leftover effluent or sludge.

Landfill gas is another potential hazard. It can migrate through the soil and cause problems ranging from odours to explosions depending on the conditions. However, it can also be tapped and burned for fuel, as is done by Cork City Council at their Kinsale Road landfill, which is a very appropriate method of dealing with what may otherwise become a potential hazard.

As the principle option for dealing with our waste in Ireland, the landfill option is not sustainable. However, as part of a national waste minimisation strategy it has several advantages to offer. The infrastructure is already in place; landfill sites are typically spacious and close to large centres of population for use as reuse/recycling depots; they can potentially be mined for future resource reclamation if needed. The lifespan of a landfill site could be extended dramatically with appropriate measures in reduction, reuse and recycling.

➤ **Incineration**

Incineration is the waste management option favoured by several local authorities around the country. As part of the planning and licensing process the EPA specifically licenses the incinerator to emit air pollution. The terms 'thermal treatment' and 'waste to energy' are both used to put a positive gloss on the burning of potentially recyclable materials. The result is airborne pollution and significant volumes of contaminated ash which still needs to be landfilled. When chlorinated plastics are burned, the inevitable result is the formation of dioxins, the most toxic substances yet known. Environmental contaminants such as dioxins are a well-documented contributor to cancer and other diseases. This is why burning them in the home or in incinerators is so dangerous. Incineration could become safer if all chlorinated plastics and many other toxics are excluded from the waste stream allowing us to recoup the heat energy from carefully screened waste. However, first it is necessary to eliminate PVC (polyvinyl chloride), other chlorine compounds and other toxics from all shop shelves and industrial processes, which is where the chain of exclusion needs to start. PVC is used for window frames, piping, shower curtains, waterproof clothing and a host of other applications. An obvious step on a personal level is to avoid PVC ourselves, which is sometimes easier said than done, but possible nonetheless.

Another factor often overlooked in the incineration debate is that when incinerators are built they need to be fed. The incentive for waste reduction vanishes in a puff of stack emissions. If we want heat, let us find environmentally sustainable methods of producing it, such as building our houses with enough insulation and draught proofing to reach 'passive standard', or using energy-efficient district heating. Even where heat from incineration can be used, it doesn't justify the continued production of an endless stream of plastic and paper waste just to feed incineration facilities.

➤ Recycling

Recycling facilities are now available for most standard household waste types. Glass, paper, card, metals, timber, compostables and plastics collection facilities operate in most counties. The different plastics – PET drink bottles, PVC piping, polythene plastic bags, polypropylene packing containers, HDPE containers and polystyrene packaging – sometimes have separate containers at recycling centres for each type. The degree of waste sorting generally depends on the collection company employed to export it. Certainly the introduction of recycling facilities in Ireland has been a welcome alternative to landfilling all our wastes. Recycling has the potential for waste reduction, as well as resource and energy conservation; however, it is a very small step towards a sustainable society.

Recycling has become the watchword in environmental education programmes; the 'my bit for the environment'. Yet it ranks well below reduction and reuse in the 'three R' hierarchy. Obviously recycling can reduce waste if the waste stream remains constant, yet in our household the generation of waste plastic shot up when collection of plastic for recycling was introduced in our area. This was because it was suddenly possible to get rid of it without landfilling it. Alternatively, if all bottles were returnable, with deposit; if all aluminium cans were just eliminated from the supply chain, as was the case in Denmark; if all unnecessary plastic was removed from supermarket shelves, then the need for recycling would be greatly reduced. It is the contents that we want, not the packaging.

Hand in hand with recycling has been the development of separation facilities in landfill sites for recyclable, toxic or awkward materials. Items such as batteries and waste electronic equipment, Christmas trees, bulbs, white goods (fridges, freezers, etc.), compostables, timber, paints, solvents, oil, construction materials and demolition wastes are all typically kept out of landfill for diversion elsewhere. Many of these are *down-cycled*, or are kept separate to minimise the toxicity of leachate. Down-cycling is the process of reusing a material for something of lower grade value, such as turning old concrete demolition waste into low grade crushed aggregate; chipping Christmas trees into bark mulch; or shredding drinks bottles into sleeping-bag padding. You end up with a lower value material rather than recycling it back into the original product, and as such you keep it out of landfill for ever (bark mulch) or at least for a little longer (sleeping-bag padding).

Where materials are exported for recycling, particularly waste electronic equipment and other mixed wastes, the potential for causing harm is great. In Africa and Asia, where many European recyclable materials end up, the toxicity of certain wastes can be very damaging to the people involved in the recycling industry. Without wanting to sound too clichéd, this work is all too often carried out by children and old people, with no comprehension of the toxicity involved in what they are doing. The ideal is to reduce our generation of waste, and to appropriately reuse what is left, not dispose of it to far-flung lands under the banner of recycling.

➤ Reuse

Reuse is more sustainable than recycling and the practice is growing. The proliferation of second-hand shops, classified newspapers and websites such as Freecycle.org demonstrates public desire for reusing things that are no longer wanted, but still useful or serviceable. Whether the motivation is financial, environmental or social, the will is evidently present to keep things moving, out of landfill and into somebody's active service.

Many industrial wastes are genuine raw materials. This doesn't necessarily stop them being dumped nor does it stop their classification as 'waste'. For example, industrial processes often generate by-products that are considered as raw materials by other industries. By keeping the different industrial wastes separate, and providing an incentive for minimisation, such wastes can be rerouted to other factories that use them. This has already been done to some extent with solvents and other wastes in Ireland and abroad, and has the potential to grow if appropriate legislative policy is introduced, such as increasing waste disposal costs for hazardous materials.

Agricultural wastes such as farmyard manure were not traditionally considered wastes, but rather valuable sources of nutrients. With changes in farming practice, this valuable resource has become a potentially polluting waste. Factory scale farming tends to lead to large quantities of liquid slurry, rather than manageable amounts of relatively dry manure. Careful nutrient management and farm practice is essential to appropriately reclassify this waste as a valuable resource once more.

➤ Dumping at sea, fly-tipping and littering

Dumping at sea, fly-tipping and littering are all practised in Ireland to a greater or lesser extent and with greater or lesser legal and social endorsement. I have read that pay-by-weight should be dropped as it was leading to fly-tipping. This is like saying that banks should leave their safes open to the public since not doing so was leading to theft and robbery.

The most obvious example of legal dumping is the disposal of toilet waste as sewage, typically after some degree of treatment. Urine and faecal matter reuse for agriculture is common in Scandinavia and many other countries where sustainability is a priority, or simply a part of daily life. Eco-toilets replace nutrients and biomass into the agricultural system, as well as eliminating the use of potable water to flush toilets, thus greatly reducing the potential for water pollution.

In terms of illegal dumping and littering, close community observation is an obvious way to begin to tackle this antisocial habit, but it is not an easy issue to address individually. The focus of this book is to help you to find ways to get rid of your own bin, rather than focusing on problems outside of your immediate control and influence.

Waste legislation in Ireland

The main items of legislation in Ireland governing household waste and waste disposal include the Waste Management Act 1996; the Environmental Protection Agency Act 1992; the European Communities Act 1972 and regulations made under these acts. There is a considerable volume of other relevant legislation. More information is available via leaflets drawn up by ENFO, Ireland's government information service on environmental matters (see appendix for contact details).

As a nation we produce far too much waste and need to deal with it in a safe and sensible fashion. If we want to embrace a sustainable future we also need to bring our waste generation to levels well below all government targets and projections.

FACE TO FACE WITH WASTE – HOUSEHOLD DISPOSAL OPTIONS EXAMINED

If you have household waste, and most of us do, then there are any number of options available for its 'disposal'. In addition to paying to have it carted away into the care of the local county council, the options include composting, burying, burning, grinding, recycling and reuse. Despite the fact that all these options are used by householders in Ireland, not all are necessarily practical, legal nor ecologically sound. They are certainly not all recommended as ways to get rid of your bin. The different disposal practices are listed below, even if only to exclude them from your list of what to do yourself. Dumping your rubbish behind the nearest tree or into the nearest river is not listed, for obvious reasons.

➤ **Paid collection**
Paid collection is the most common option. Hand over your money, your waste and also your vote as to how the world should be. If it suits you, then you probably haven't got as far as reading this. If it doesn't, read on. That said, if you cancel your collection service but keep your old plastic bin and use it to store the small volume of wastes

that are really difficult to dispose of in other ways, then even your bin has something to contribute.

➤ Burning
Burning of waste is illegal in Ireland – unless you have a licence. The burning of chlorinated plastics generates dioxins and is toxic, whether in a licensed incinerator or in your fireplace. However, if you have clean timber, without paint or varnish, and non-glossy plain paper that is no longer useful, it makes sense to use it as firelighters. Grill-pan fat that has been wrapped in paper also makes an excellent firelighter and removes a difficult 'waste' from the bin.

➤ Burying
Burying is not really a suitable method of disposal for most waste, although if you have construction and demolition (C&D) waste and a new driveway to construct then it makes perfect sense to use the clean C&D waste as fill for the base of the drive. Concrete blocks, broken concrete and brick are ideally suited to this task, where they would otherwise contribute to waste disposal costs and volume. This has the added advantage of avoiding the use of virgin materials such as gravel or hardcore as the base layer. Burying is also suitable for wastes such as dog and cat litter, which can contribute to garden nutrients while reducing your bin weight. Choose an area that will be left well alone for the foreseeable future, such as under non-food shrubs or trees.

➤ Grinding

Grinding of waste in kitchen sink garbage grinders is not a recommended way to minimise your waste load, because it merely converts solid waste to water pollution. Not only that, but it takes the very waste that is easily compostable and literally pours your potential garden nutrients down the drain.

➤ Recycling

Recycling, or more correctly 'delivery to the recycling centre for down-cycling or export and reprocessing abroad' is another option. From a sustainability perspective it should be viewed with some suspicion and used for wastes that cannot otherwise be reused or just kept out of the house to begin with. It is much better to avoid plastic in the shops than to cart it off to China for melting down into fence-posts (or whatever they do with it in China). Consumer demand does change company practice, so instead of recycling your beverage cans at great energy costs, start demanding returnable bottles like many sensible European countries.

➤ Composting

Composting all organics is not only possible; it is the best method of recouping the nutrients in your food and garden wastes and of minimising your bin weight. Compostables are a particularly heavy and smelly element of your waste and have the potential to leak out into your car on the way to the dump on your six-monthly visits there once you cancel your bin collection. Good composting converts all these potential problems into top-quality garden soil for growing the best fruit and vegetables in the neighbourhood – thus cutting down further on plastic supermarket packaging.

➤ Reuse

Reuse is the ultimate 'disposal' option, hand in hand with reduction in the first instance. For items that have outgrown their usefulness, reusing them is the only sensible and sustainable route to take. When it comes to the basics, such as jars and glass bottles, a return policy would be a great help. However, in the short-term absence of helpful infrastructure, reusing what you can in terms of the weekly shop is a good start, combined with judicious purchasing habits. Shopping at the local market and using a cardboard box or cloth bags can generate infinitely less plastic than a supermarket selection of the same basic ingredients, which are usually fresher and better quality too. For items such as furniture, books, boot-scrapers and, as in the *Wind in the Willows* 'a plaster bust of Queen Victoria', second-hand shops, new home owners, and friends and family are good recipients of unwanted but potentially useful 'waste'. Don't dump it onto them though, or it will go straight into their bin, which isn't exactly the idea.

LOOKING IN THE BIN

Once you have examined your weekly bin with the above measures in mind, there is usually very little left over. If you do choose to pay for collection then check the most suitable method of reduction for your needs and for your area. Collection facilities vary greatly from place to place. Some areas have no commercial collection facilities available, others have council collection, while some have private contractors. Some services include collection of recyclables, with the range of recyclables collected varying according to the company involved.

Payment also varies with each area, although some form of volume or weight measurement is now more common than standing charges. Nonetheless, if you get your waste down to one carrier bag per week, the bin charge will probably be considerably greater than if you deliver it to the dump yourself. If you are keeping waste for landfill, an old wheelie bin is the ideal receptacle. Remember to keep food waste and unwashed food packaging out, or sealed, to avoid rodents, smells and leakages.

In addition to bin charges there are now charges at the source of purchasing for items such as fridges, washing machines and other 'white goods'. In time, source charges may become effective for other difficult or toxic wastes such as batteries, asbestos, CFL bulbs and fluorescent lights. Along with solvents, paints and other hazardous household wastes it is already forbidden to place these items in your domestic bin. Such source charges are a good way of ensuring that the infrastructure is in place for the safe disposal of difficult wastes. However, reduction by avoiding these is better still, and can be employed directly in each purchasing decision. I am not advocating candles rather than CFL bulbs, but buying only rechargeable batteries is a very easy way to dramatically reduce your hazardous battery waste. Of course, avoiding battery-operated equipment works better still ... Check the eco-shops in the appendices for hand-operated torches, radios and other appliances.

Reduction isn't outlined in the above section because it isn't a disposal option – it is considerably better than disposal, and is outlined in more detail later. Keep it in mind, and let your imagination roam while you are asleep or daydreaming – to become an environmentally sustainable society, as well as just getting rid of our bins, we will need to set our imaginations loose.

WHAT TO DO IF YOU DON'T DUMP?

Clearly the least favourable option for waste is to dump it. Whether it goes to landfill or to incineration, dumping is without doubt a waste of resources for society and money for you.

Reduce, Reuse, Recycle is all well and good as an aspiration, but if it were practised and applied to all levels of society this book would not be necessary, and we still have room for improvement. A more thorough version could be summarised as follows:

1. **Eliminate**.
2. **Substitute** for a more sustainable alternative.
3. **Reduce**.
4. **Reuse** (this requires care at the manufacturing and purchasing stage as well as simply in the home).
5. **Compost** all kitchen and garden waste that is organic in nature.
6. **Recycle** (making the same thing again).
7. **Down-cycle** (making into something else).
8. **Recoup energy** via 'waste to energy' incineration (Clean paper and clean timber only. Do *not* burn wood composites, plastics, laminates, coloured or glossy paper or treated wood).

9. **'Dump'** should be listed, not because it is a desirable end step, but because it exists as a waste management option, whether or not it should. For some difficult wastes, until the manufacturing processes support greater sustainability, landfilling is the most appropriate containment method available.

Reduction of our waste *intake* for each item in our bin is the aim. Elimination of all waste sources is not really possible, but it is surprising how quickly you discover that such and such an essential household item is actually quite dispensable. Once I bought toothpaste that advertised 'no sodium bicarbonate, no surfactants, no chemicals'. I bought it and used half of it. Then I discovered that water, which also has no sodium bicarbonate, no surfactants and no chemicals tasted nicer and did just as good a job. That was about ten years ago and my teeth seem to be doing fine!

Reuse could have a 'down-use' entry after it on the list. Reusing glass bottles for milk is common practice on the continent, just as it used to be here. It is far better than recycling because it only requires washing to make the product fit for reuse, instead of vast energy inputs in crushing, melting and remanufacturing the glass. Using old yoghurt cartons for freezing your chicken stock is really down-use rather than reuse, because it never sends the old waste product back to the factory for refilling. Using waste containers around the home instead of buying freezer bags and plastic cartons is useful insofar as we avoid buying new empty plastic containers and then dumping perfectly serviceable ones. However, we will never stem the constant tide of waste unless we stop buying items that come in non-returnable containers.

So, remember the essentials:

Step 1   Be ruthless when shopping

Step 2   Compost what you can

Step 3   Reuse everything

Stepping into Step 1
Being Ruthless When Shopping

Take some time to really look at your weekly shopping. Notice how many things are there that you do not need or even want. There may be nets for the oranges; plastic around the bread; multiple layers that appear to be necessary to contain pizzas, chocolates, sweets, toiletries and a host of other 'essential items'. All these wrappings are surplus to your requirements, why pay for them twice? Once to buy and a second time to throw away. Three times even, if you consider the environmental costs. Even items that benefit from packaging, such as milk, eggs and flour, could easily be bought in returnable containers if the infrastructure were in place.

Avoiding the supermarket route is the easiest way to sidestep the packaging mountain. Small local suppliers generally sell fruit and vegetables loose rather than packaged. Local farmers' markets are becoming more common all around the country. Suppliers of local produce either cannot afford expensive packaging, or simply do not waste their time and resources on it. Return the egg boxes to your local supplier; if you live in the country, buy your milk from a farming neighbour in a reusable container, and pasteurise it yourself if you prefer (see Seymour, 2003, in the further reading for how to do this). At least flour comes in a plain paper bag that can be used as a firelighter when you are finished with it.

All money-saving manuals warn against impulse buys, which are often unnecessary and not always even wanted. Just ask the quick question with each purchase: how exactly am I going to dispose of this product/ container when I am finished with it? For example, a plastic picnic bench may have a longer life expectancy than a chocolate wrapper, but it also takes up more space in a landfill site when its useful lifespan ends. One of the recommended ways to overcome the draw of advertising and impulse buys is to make a shopping list beforehand and to purchase only what is on that list.

The recommendation here is not penury, it is making conscious choices. Cutting out the extraneous, the unnecessary and the unwanted shouldn't be a difficult thing to defend. However, the weight of advertising is geared towards selling people exactly the opposite. Much of what we do in the world is unconscious. We don't *mean* to alter global weather patterns when we buy our new cars and virgin paper products and a myriad of other consumer items, but unless we reverse current trends in our resource use that will be the result. By making conscious, informed choices we can overcome many of the environmental and social challenges that currently face us, as well as reducing our bin charges.

Seeing the connection between what we purchase and what we pay in terms of disposal is a matter of re-educating ourselves, and then changing our habits to reflect what we want. If you are health conscious you will know the implications of including sugar and saturated fats in the diet. However, most people who know this still choose to buy a bar of chocolate occasionally. You can see the connection between your overall health and the frequency of ingesting such foods. Similarly a simple change in mindset can help us see the waste implications of our purchases. Consider more than just cost and bin charges when you buy. At face value it is difficult to see the difference between Fairtrade goods and ordinary products, yet the difference exists for the farmers who grow the cocoa beans, sugar cane and other crops. Our shopping habits echo around the planet, either helping to create the world we want or going against the values we espouse, depending on what we choose to purchase.

Being ruthless when shopping does not always mean making the cheapest purchase. In fact the contrary is often the case. Some things will be more expensive, but many people find they actually save money on their over-all shopping basket. Shopping with this awareness means that you look for products that you genuinely want to have in your life and products, for example of Fairtrade origin, that do more good in the world than harm. Watching the volume of waste is only a springboard to this awareness about how you spend your money. If money talks, then how you spend yours is a direct way to voice your decision on what happens in the world.

When you are shopping, remember that the items that go into your basket all need to leave your house again in one way or another. If you fill your basket with things that can be composted, reused, easily maintained and repaired or else recycled, then you can be sure that you won't be paying for their disposal as well as for their purchase. Try shopping *really* ruthlessly for a month and see how it reduces your waste.

Stepping into Step 2
Composting

Composting has very definitely moved from being the sole domain of the gardening fanatic to a basic ecological (and cash-saving) activity. This is not a definitive book on household composting, but the different basic types of composting are outlined, with references and contacts for learning more.

'Composting is easy' is the refrain from councils and environmental groups alike, and once you get down to it, you will also find that there is always space for experimentation and improvement.

There are several different types of composting:

- Thermophilic composting
- Anaerobic composting
- Vermicomposting
- Trench composting
- Bokashi composting
- Plastic compost bins

Each method has its pros and cons. It is likely that no single system will fulfil all your requirements, but a combination of two or more systems may work perfectly. What follows is a list of the different composting types and where they may be applicable. Try one or two that seem to suit your garden conditions and your own resources, and be prepared to try something else the following year if the first choice does not produce the results you want.

➤ **Thermophilic composting**

Thermophilic composting is the standard aerated compost-heap composting. This system of composting relies on the activity of heat and bacteria and other soil organisms to break down organic material into rich dark compost. The necessary ingredients are air, moisture and a good mix of 'green' and 'brown' organic waste, as outlined below. This system needs some skill and care for it to work properly, as well as strength for the occasional turning. Rodents and flies can be a problem if food waste is included.

The site for the compost heap should be easily accessible and preferably in the sun. It should be directly on the ground, to allow micro-organisms and worms to enter and exit as they wish. The standard design for keeping a compost heap in a tidy shape is some sort of timber unit about 1 metre cubed. This can be anything from three pallets tied together to form the back and sides, to a purpose-built stacking frame of timber squares, each unit being about 15 centimetres high. Concrete blocks or plywood also work or just an open heap will suffice if you have the space and don't mind the untidiness.

A compost heap is best made in one go, with 10-15 centimetre-thick layers of the different materials. Starting at the bottom layer, use sticks and twigs to allow air circulation. Next, put in decomposed organic matter, such as rotted manure or old compost, to activate the heap. Follow this with layers of kitchen waste if you are using it, garden weedings, straw, paper, leaves or grass cuttings. Alternate the green and brown waste to avoid an excessive thickness of any one type of material, and a sprinkle of lime is sometimes useful to control acidity.

Greens include nitrogen-rich materials such as:	Browns include fibre rich materials such as:
grass clippings (add in small amounts only)	fallen leaves, tough plant stalks
fleshy leaves such as nettles and comfrey	cardboard, egg boxes, crumpled newspaper
young weeds and plants, poultry manure (without the fibrous bedding material)	thin woody prunings, straw

There are also intermediate materials that do not really qualify as either green or brown, but are perfect in the compost heap. These include food scraps, tea bags and coffee grounds, cut flowers, animal bedding from farm animals and herbivorous pets such as rabbits, tough green leaves such as rhubarb and bracken and the poultry manure *with* the carbonaceous bedding material. These should be used to form separate layers within the compost heap.

Compost activators can be bought to kick-start or speed up the process, but if good nitrogen-rich material such as poultry manure or comfrey is in the heap, it should work fine. Urine is a very effective activator, being high in nitrogen. Apply at night, or out of sight, for minimum disturbance!

Once the heap is built, water lightly and cover with a piece of cardboard, plastic or carpet (without the under-lay, which tends to break apart after a while). Ensure that the heap does not dry out, as this will limit the growth of the appropriate micro-organisms. The centre of the heap should generate a lot of heat, so check this every so often with a garden fork. Skewer the heap and leave the fork for a minute, then withdraw it and feel the prongs with your hand to check the temperature. Once the heap begins to cool down, after weeks or months depending on the ingredients, turn it once. This is laborious, but helps to mix the outer layers to the centre and to ensure a good kill-off of weeds and diseases. When this new heap has cooled and you have a rich dark soil, work this finished compost into vegetable beds or use to mulch around fruit bushes or shrubs. It won't look like peat moss unless you sieve it, but this isn't necessary to get good growing results in the garden.

Thermophilic composting is a good method of making nutrient-rich compost if you have the space and commitment, but is not necessarily the most appropriate method for small gardens, for non-gardeners or for food waste.

➤ Anaerobic composting

If turning sounds like too much hard work then you can build an anaerobic compost heap. This is essentially a heap of organic waste from the garden and kitchen, preferably layered, piled up to 3 or 4 feet high. This is topped with an inch of soil and a cover such as old carpet. The heap is then left to rot down into the soil.

There are a few drawbacks to this system as compared to thermophilic composting. It is slower, taking up to a year to break down. It is generally colder and more acidic, so lime may be needed in the garden to regulate the pH. It does not break down weed seeds or perennial roots. The fibrous elements do not break down as much, so it tends to be strawy and rough, and it may attract flies if not adequately covered.

This is a suitable method for those with enough space to leave the heap idle for the year and has the advantage of being less work than most compost systems. Some storage of kitchen waste is necessary before adding as a layer to the heap, so this composting method may need to be carried out in conjunction with a plastic bin or old rubbish bin or with a Bokashi composting system to prevent flies and odours, and limit rodents. Alternatively use for garden waste only and have a separate kitchen composting system.

➤ Vermicomposting

Worm Eat My Garbage was the book by biologist Mary Appelhof that introduced many people to the art and science of worm composting. Build an environment in which the correct worms have the time of their lives: eating, breeding and making lots and lots of rich vermicompost: that is a one-line description of a very technical home science.

Lots of sources of information exist to explain vermicomposting step-by-step. The Irish Peatland Conservation Council website espouses it as one of many alternatives to peat moss. Organic gardening books are another good source of information and can be found in any good library.

The container is the first step with a worm bin. A converted rubbish bin will do fine, as will a purpose-built timber box system. Alternatively there are a number of purpose-designed systems on the market such as the 'Can O' Worms'. Worm composting can be done indoors or outdoors, so apartment living is no excuse not to give it a go.

Whatever design you adopt, the worm bin should be quite robust, well drained (yet contain the liquid if it is indoors or if you want to use the nutrient-rich solution as a fertiliser), ventilated and yet sufficiently sealed to eliminate rodents and flies. If you are using it indoors, it should be sealed enough to keep in the worms and liquid. The worm bin should also be easy to use, both for filling and emptying. Timber boxes should be made of untreated wood.

First, choose a bin, or make a box, with ample drainage. Cover the base with gravel to further facilitate drainage and then cover with perforated plastic to prevent the compost mixing with the gravel. Place the 'bedding' material on this; a mixture of 50 per cent shredded, soaked newspaper and 50 per cent compost, rotted manure or leaf mould. A handful of soil, crushed limestone, sand or, I am told, sweepings from the kitchen floor, apparently aids the worms' digestion.

A 'recycled worm farm' is recommended by Christchurch City Council in New Zealand. This uses four old tyres placed one on top of the other, sitting on a piece of corrugated metal sheeting. This system has the advantage of being well insulated for the winter and also appears to be rat-proof, which is key, not least because the rats will eat your worms. For a large household you would need two or three stacks of tyres, because it is important not to let the uneaten food build up.

Another advantage to this system is that the bottom tyre can be slid out for removing the compost. Then, when emptied, it can be placed back on top of the heap. If you have the recycled worm farm sitting on an impervious surface you will need to collect the liquid. Dilute this

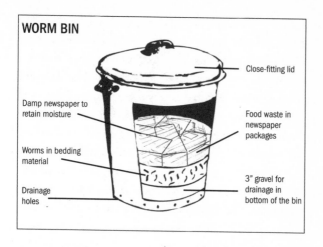

WORM BIN

Close-fitting lid

Damp newspaper to retain moisture

Food waste in newspaper packages

Worms in bedding material

Drainage holes

3" gravel for drainage in bottom of the bin

to make an excellent liquid feed for tomatoes or other hungry plants.

Whatever design you choose, site your worm bin out of direct sunshine and not in a frost pocket or an exposed windy area. The worms thrive best at temperatures between 18 and 25°C. In winter the worm bin may need to be brought into a heated greenhouse or shed if you want to keep the worms working for you throughout the year. Having said that, I have seen worm composting systems working well in Irish conditions year round, with just a slight slow-down in winter. Another factor when siting the worm bin is the location of the kitchen. The worm bin needs to be as easily accessible as possible, not a day's march through the garden, unless you would welcome the excuse to escape for a few minutes …

Next you need to find the worms, about 250-500

grammes (or if you are counting, anywhere between 100 and 1,000 depending on the size of the worms and the source of information you follow). The ones used for worm composting are those that thrive on rotting organic matter, so look first to a nearby horse-manure heap or an existing worm bin or compost heap. Brandling or tiger worms (*Eisenia foetida*) are the usual species used. These are commonly sold for bait, so fishing shops are another port of call if neighbourhood supplies are limited. They are also sold by suppliers of worms and composting equipment. Check the Irish Peatland Conservation Council website in the appendices for an up-to-date contacts list.

Add the worms to the bedding material and cover with a good layer of pre-soaked newspaper to retain warmth and moisture and to keep the bin dark. Now you are ready to begin adding the food. A converted rubbish bin-sized system will take most of the kitchen waste from about two people, so a bigger bin, more bins, or some additional type of compost system is needed for larger households.

At feeding time, a number of pointers are helpful. A mixed diet is best for the worms, so add shredded newspaper and leafy garden waste occasionally. Add food only when the worms need it, rather than when the kitchen storage bin is full, so 'little and often' is the way to proceed. The food can be added in pockets in amongst the bedding material or as a partial layer of less than 5 centimetres over the surface. The advice on what to avoid changes from list to list, but generally avoid anything non-organic in nature such as glass, metal, ceramic and the like, as well as seeding weeds, diseased plants, fish/meat/dairy, large amounts of citrus, bought flowers and dog and cat faeces.

The worms like to remain covered while they are working for you. The usual recommendation for this is to use damp cardboard or newspaper. I find that this can be tricky to lift after a while as it begins to tear, and it just adds messiness to the job. What works really well is to wrap the kitchen food waste in newspaper and just drop that straight into the worm bin. The worms will work their way up through the base of the newspaper as it becomes moist from below, while avoiding ever having food, or worms, exposed on the surface. This reduces flies and odours. Take care with this method not to overload your worm bin, which is important to keep it working well. Dig into the bin occasionally to check that the worms are keeping up to date with the food being added.

Maintenance includes feeding, checking and emptying. Worms can survive for 4 or 5 weeks without new food, so there is no need to stockpile before the holidays. Check the worm bin every couple of weeks to make sure the moisture balance is right. Water if it is too dry; add shredded paper or cardboard if it is too wet and address the drainage problem. Check the worms too, that they are thriving and happy with the type of food being added, and the amount. There shouldn't be much of a smell, so odours indicate that too much food is being added and is beginning to rot, which the worms don't like. Reduce your food input to the bin if this is happening, to let the worms catch up. Surface area is the key to having enough capacity, so add another bin if the worms are overloaded. Checking with a small garden fork also aerates the bin, which helps to keep everything healthy. Too much citrus rind can lead to acidic conditions, and if this is suspected then stop applying them and add crushed egg shells or crushed limestone for alkalinity.

Although the worms reduce the volume of waste considerably, emptying will be necessary at some stage. There are a number of ways to do it. If you have a low, flat box, press the contents to one side and add the new food at the other side. Over time the worms will migrate into the new food and the old compost can be removed. For larger bins the recommendation is to place their favourite food on the top layer for a week (presumably it takes a bit of observation to get to know them that well) and then remove this complete with worms to some buckets. Empty out the compost and then begin the worm bin again using the contents of the buckets as the new starting worms and bedding.

You can treat the resulting compost like concentrated fertiliser, owing to both its high nutrient content and relatively limited volume. It can be used as a surface dressing for pot plants or patio planters; sprinkled into seed drills or mixed with compost to enhance moisture-holding capacity. Some sources cite it as being unsuitable to use alone in pots and seed trays since it may be too rich for seed germination. If you collect the liquid from beneath the worm bin this can be used as a fertiliser, diluted to the colour of weak tea before use.

For our own kitchen food waste we use a wheelie bin turned into a wormery. There are two of these side by side, with food added alternately between them and they are working fine to date. From giving environmental talks and lectures I have noticed that some people are reluctant to use a worm system on account of the worms themselves. If you are a bit squeamish, ask for help from a friend or neighbour or buy an off-the-shelf, easy maintenance system, because they have a lot to offer in terms of reducing your kitchen waste and producing excellent compost in a completely rodent-free way.

> ## Trench composting

This is a fairly straightforward method of converting organic kitchen waste into soil. Basically dig a trench in the garden and add the vegetable peelings and other kitchen organics to it a bucket at a time. After each application, cover over with soil to prevent flies or odours being a nuisance. When the spring arrives, plant courgettes, beans or other hungry plants over the trench. These will make best use of the nutrients generated by the decomposing material, and the following year the trench will be ready for other crops. This is suitable for regular gardeners with enough space, but may be a bit troublesome for others. Rodents can be a problem unless you earth up quite well or use Bokashi (see below section on Bokashi composting), which makes the food waste unpalatable to them.

This method is a good solution for dealing with occasional compost fiascos. If your chosen composting method didn't work as well as you had expected, then laying the resulting material in a trench and planting with hungry plants is an excellent way to recoup the nutrients and deal with the compost. It can also be used for pet waste, but only in non-food growing areas. Burying food waste or pet waste with soil to a depth of 18 inches is reported to virtually eliminate all odour and rodent problems.

➤ Bokashi composting

Effective micro-organisms (EM) are naturally occurring bacteria, fungi and yeasts in a balanced combination that can be used to enhance the health of soil, plants, water, humans and animals. EM functions in the compost in much the same way as yoghurt does in the intestines, enhancing the action of the natural bacteria. Bokashi is the name given to bran that has been mixed with EM solution.

With this form of composting the Bokashi is sprinkled onto organic kitchen waste in an air-tight Bokashi composting bucket. The food waste must be squashed down into the bucket to minimise aeration because the EM needs anaerobic conditions to thrive. Liquid generated by the mixture percolates through the bucket and can be drained off. This liquid is high in nutrients and effective micro-organisms, and when diluted makes an excellent liquid feed for the garden. It is also a good septic tank activator and drain degreaser, so it can also just be poured down the sink neat if your garden has drunk its fill.

The compost material ferments rather than breaking down. In doing so, the mixture becomes unpalatable to flies and rodents, so it can be buried in trenches in the garden directly or can be added to a compost heap in layers, apparently without attracting pests. By digging the Bokashi treated waste into the garden you get the benefits of the nutrients from the waste as well as the benefits of the EM in the soil. This type of system is best for households with enough tilled garden to dig in the treated waste. Alternatively if you have gardening neighbours or an allotment, the treated waste is an active bonus for the soil – and the flowers and vegetables growing in it. The Bokashi bran mix can be made up at home or can be purchased from a supplier (check the appendices for details).

➤ Plastic Compost Bins

There is a growing variety of plastic compost bins on the market, available from garden centres, garden suppliers and county councils. They have been listed here as a separate entry because they do not fit neatly into any of the above categories. Plastic bins are generally used for kitchen waste since garden clippings and weedings are usually too bulky for them.

There are a number of different design types with corresponding differences in price and effectiveness:

- Rotating bins
- 'Green Cone'-type bins
- Standard plastic compost bins
- Others

Rotating bins

Rotating bins are free standing or wall-mounted bins that can be turned to aerate the contents. Examples include the Big Pig and Tumbler composters. These tend to be relatively expensive, but are rodent-proof and advertise excellent results and ease of use. They tend to be good for small urban gardens, anywhere where mess and rodents are particularly undesirable or where ease of use is a priority.

The 'Green Cone'

The 'Green Cone' has a lattice basket base that is buried in the ground (as distinct from the standard flat-bottomed plastic compost bins). These function as a kitchen organic waste disposal method rather than a way to get good compost. Bacteria digest the food waste and earthworms drag the compost out into the surrounding soil, building it up and fertilising the garden near the bin.

These are a good solution for holiday homes with infrequent occupancy and minimum maintenance opportunity, or for small gardens where mess and rodents are undesirable. They are limited in the amount of compost that they process, and occasional emptying is necessary to remove excess material. This can be used as a layer in an aerobic compost heap or in a garden compost trench. Depending on what goes into the bin, use any removed material with due caution. Because they are a disposal unit rather than a composting unit they can, according to their manufacturers, be used for fish, meat, poultry, bones, bread, pasta, soup, curry, fruit including peelings, vegetables including peelings, dairy produce, cooked food scraps, crushed egg shells, tea bags and animal excrement.

Standard plastic compost bins

Standard plastic compost bins are the most commonly used, but are not always as straightforward to operate as they seem. My personal experience with these compost bins, with or without a perforated base, is that they have the potential to produce a relatively sludgy mess unless they are turned and aerated. They can also attract rats, although some newer designs may be limiting this. A New Zealander friend, with a lifetime of agricultural research behind him, told me that he lets the rats turn the compost in his bin and then poisons them, which seems somewhat ungrateful. Nonetheless rats can carry the potentially fatal Weil's disease and should be kept well away from the kitchen garden.

These bins have the potential to be good for urban or rural gardens, being tidy and inexpensive. The best results I have seen are where rat poison was left near the bin, leaving the worms in peace to do an excellent job of turning the compost. However, rat poison can in turn poison animals further up the food chain such as owls and hawks, so many people avoid it on wildlife and environmental grounds. If you find that the plastic bin doesn't give the results you want, use it for less rodent-tasty food such as citrus peels, onion skins and the like to keep these out of the main worm bins. Then just bury the compost in a trench system when the bin fills and grow courgettes and broad beans. Alternatively use the contents of the bin as a layer or two within a new aerobic or anaerobic compost heap.

Other bins

Other bins are coming on the market all the time, now that composting is becoming so attractive. The Earth-maker is a new system from New Zealand, in which the compost is turned as it moves slowly down through the bin. The design of the standard free-standing bins varies occasionally, producing greater rodent-proofing, different sizes and so on. Before you choose a bin yourself, search online or visit some friends and see what they have found to work.

Composting conclusions

If at first you don't succeed, remember that it is still cheaper to try again than to throw in the gardening trowel and pay the bin-collector to remove this heavy, bulky element of your household waste. Whatever compost you produce will be better than landfill. I remember hearing with fascination some time ago that a sample of excavated landfill material about 30 years old contained, among other exciting items, an intact, if somewhat limp lettuce that had been preserved by the anaerobic conditions. Any attempt at composting will be an improvement on that.

Composting is an excellent way to reduce your bin weight, your bin volume and your environmental impact. From a sustainability perspective it is pretty much obligatory; returning nutrients and organic matter back to the soil from which it came. If you are hesitant and you want to see how much you would save on weight, place your food waste in separate bags for few weeks, weigh it separately and calculate your savings for the year. For that matter, just try the system that looks easiest and then see how much you save.

What to do with compost: the square foot garden plan

If you find that you have lots of wonderful compost and no way to utilise it because your garden is too small, now is your chance to shine: a square foot garden is an ideal way to introduce children to gardening or to begin gardening yourself if you haven't done much of it before. It is also great for small urban gardens with the minimum of space. The square foot garden fits into an area 1.2 x 1.2 metres and is divided into sixteen plots of 1 square foot each. Each plot is planted with a different type of vegetable or herb. Gardening in some way, any way at all really, is the best method to utilise the compost that you generate from your kitchen and garden organics.

To start your own square foot garden, choose an area in a sunny position on relatively free-draining ground. The closer it is to the house the more you will get to tending it and harvesting from it. Build a timber frame with four untreated boards of about 15 x 3 x 120 centimetres. Lay overlapping layers of newspapers or cardboard on the base to suppress existing grass and weeds. Fill the frame with a mixture of compost and good loamy soil. The author of *Square Foot Gardening*, Mel Bartholomew, recommends peat moss as well, but I try to avoid this since it contributes to the destruction of native peatland habitats, which are important wildlife areas and a very valuable carbon sink for reducing climate change. He also recommends avoiding soil, since this carries weeds and is not as rich as compost, but I don't see the harm in including it if you are prepared to do a small amount of weeding afterwards. Mark out the 1.2 x 1.2 metre bed into sixteen square-foot plots with string, plastic or light timber. Next you are ready to plant.

Plant a different vegetable, herb or flower in each plot, using the appropriate number of plants or seeds for each type. This depends on their final size. For example, nine garlic bulbs, one potato, six cabbages (thinned to one or two as they grow), three broad beans and so on. As the plants mature, eat the thinnings. So surplus beetroot seedlings, for example, can be eaten in salads, while the remaining four can be left to mature. As each square-foot plot is harvested in turn, add more compost before planting the next crop of a different type of plant.

If you want to maximise the use of space, you can grow seedlings in trays so that they have a head start by the time they go into the bed. Plant taller plants and climbers on the north edge of the bed, to avoid shading the rest of the plots. Harvest each crop as soon as it is ready and begin the next crop immediately. The *HDRA* (now called Garden Organic) *Encyclopaedia of Organic Gardening* gives a description of what plants to place where for year-round productivity, and is well worth reading if you want to get growing.

Stepping into Step 3
Reusing Everything

When it comes to reducing the amount of stuff that ends up in your bin at the end of the week, it makes sense to reuse everything that you possibly can. In this context I am taking a fairly broad definition of reuse, including rerouting and recycling as well, although the more direct the reuse the better. Direct reuse includes fixing broken things, using second-hand shops, charity shops, eBay, Buy and Sell, Freecycle.org or LETS.* Alternatively, appropriately pass on to others who can make good use of it. Reuse of returnables such as milk bottles and glass yoghurt pots is something that will become more

* LETS – Local Exchange Trading Systems or Schemes – are defined by letslink uk (www.letslinkuk.net) as 'local community-based mutual aid networks in which people exchange all kinds of goods and services with one another, without the need for money'.

common again as our society chooses to adopt more sustainable practices, as demonstrated by other more environmentally minded European countries.

➤ Reusing things yourself

The most obvious person to reuse the things you have is you. Making a habit of using refillable containers and avoiding disposables is the first step. But stepping back further from reuse, there is actually another step and another whole philosophy in this consumer culture: properly maintaining the things we already have and fixing the things that break. Whether it is a computer printer, a bicycle or a Christmas decoration, if you fix it then there is no need to dump it and replace it.

Even if it is beyond using as is, why dump it just because it has fulfilled its original purpose? Reuse can just as easily apply to using large yoghurt cartons as freezer containers; reusing old carpet off-cuts as compost heap covers; reusing untreated timber off-cuts as kindling for starting the fire and so on *ad infinitum*.

➤ Rerouting Elsewhere

Rerouting applies to anything that you can sell or give away for *appropriate* reuse elsewhere. This is not an excuse for a dumping frenzy on your cousins with the new house, or for donations of moth-eaten blankets to an aid appeal. Many household 'waste' items are merely objects that have outlived their wantedness in the house and are taking up valuable storage space. Rather than dump your cider-making kit, your old Lego or Uncle Fred's tea-set, find a suitable home for it. Try selling it, or else let it go to someone who can. Check your friends and family too. You never know, maybe your cousins are in need of a sofa or a baby's cot. Babies' clothes are particularly good at doing the rounds.

Freecycle.org is another way to reroute the things you no longer need and want to move on to a new home. Increasing numbers of communities in Ireland are using the Freecycle.org website for their local area to keep things moving around for free. It helps to cut down on clutter, reduce new purchases and associated resource consumption, and minimise the amount of dumping that goes on.

➤ Returnables

Glass milk bottles, glass yoghurt pots, returnable beverage bottles and sturdy packing boxes are all examples of returnable packaging items that were once commonly routed straight back to the suppliers. Dumping these into our landfills and incinerators doesn't make much sense, not least because glass doesn't provide much heat! Ask your usual supplier to stock returnables and to take them back again. Health food shops are usually good about facilitating you where possible, sometimes offering a refill service for detergent containers and washing-up liquids.

Even where retailers are unable or unwilling to provide a returnables service, there are still ways to employ it successfully. Jam jars are a typical example because those who make jams and preserves are often happy to be given dozens of them, year after year.

➤ Recycling

For things beyond repair, reuse or rerouting, recycling is the next step. From a sustainability perspective view this as a last resort rather than the first step. Materials that are generally easily sent for recycling include glass, paper, metal, textiles, compostables and plastics.

- **Glass:** This needs to be sorted by colour to preserve colour differences in the recycled product. Glass recycling is considerably less energy intensive than manufacture from raw silica and other ingredients. Industrial-scale reuse is still the best option, since re-use requires only washing and delivery to source for refilling and recapping. Shops and supermarkets on the continent have returnable glass bottles, jars, glass yoghurt pots and the like, that are reused directly by the food manufacturer for minimum environmental impact. Only by requesting these will they become available, so keep asking your usual supplier to stock them.

- **Paper:** Different grades are often recycled separately as paper, card or newsprint. It is even better to get the maximum use out of any given piece of paper, such as using both sides, before recycling. Office A4 printer paper can be reused directly if the reverse side is not specifically confidential. This is termed 'printer scrap', in our house and stored carefully for printing drafts, lists and the like. Envelopes can be reused by purchasing reuse labels from your favourite charity, or by printing off your own logo on an A5 sticker and writing the new postal address on that, or by simply crossing out the old name and address and clearly writing the new one. A creative use for scrap paper is to use it to make your own hand-made paper for use in craft projects. Information on this is usually available in the craft section of your local library.

- **Metals:** These usually need to be sorted into aluminium and ferric metals (i.e. containing iron – a magnet will tell you quickly which is which by sticking to ferric metals, with iron in them, and not to non-ferric metals). Usually beverage cans are aluminium while food tins are ferric. Generally metals are easily recyclable, and facilities are relatively common. There is a high potential for dioxin and other toxin production during the recycling process if chlorinated products such as plastics are in the mix. Because of this, ensure that plastic-coated electric wiring and other plastics are not put into the metal recycling bin.

- **Textiles:** Clothes and textiles can be collected for second-hand shops or for export by charities such as Enable Ireland, or can be down-cycled for rags. Some recycling centres also have a textile collection depot.

- **Compostables:** See Stepping into Step 2 on page 50 for more detail. Increasingly municipal composting is available at recycling centres, so make enquiries. They often have a list of excluded wastes, so follow the house rules to ensure that the service remains available to the public. Keep in mind though that home composting means you get to keep the nutrients in your own garden, and it minimises hauling which reduces your carbon footprint.

- **Plastics** come in a whole variety of colours, grades and types. Some are recyclable, others are not, depending on the type of plastic. The most common form of plastic 'recycling' is down-cycling from the original product into a lower grade product. The different types of plastics are sometimes labelled with their recycling code, which makes for easier sorting. In practice, how you sort plastics in your home will ideally reflect the requirements of your local recycling centre, thereby making your trips there quicker and easier.

The different plastic types are listed below. The number given is the recycling code, printed on the base of the container. The examples are indicative only, because the versatility of plastics means that the different types can be made into lots of different things.

- PET/PETE No. 1 – polyethylene terthalate; e.g. clear or tinted drink bottles.
- HDPE No. 2 – high-density polyethylene; e.g. heavy-duty liner materials, plastic milk jugs, plastic bags.
- PVC No. 3 – polyvinyl chloride; e.g. PVC windows, guttering etc. Highly toxic when burned, producing dioxins.

- LDPE No. 4 – low-density polyethylene; e.g. milk container lids, frozen food bags.
- PP No. 5 – polypropylene; e.g. woven ground-cover plastic; coal bags; squeezy ketchup bottles.
- PS No. 6 – polystyrene; e.g. insulation, meat trays, disposable cups.
- Other No. 7 – Multi-layer plastics and plastics other than the six typical types.

To further complicate the recycling process, different plastic types are often used in the one product, such as HDPE lids and seals on PET bottles. Different recycling facilities accept different plastic depending on the companies that collect their materials. One thing to remember is that if plastics are not adequately washed and sorted then a whole container load of materials may be rejected by the collection company and dumped into landfill, so follow the recycling centre guidelines and simultaneously press your local council for more varied facilities if some types are not catered for locally.

- **Timber:** Clean timber is accepted for chipping in many landfill sites. Timber is quite versatile and adaptable for reusing if you are good at DIY. Smaller bits of untreated and unpainted timber can be used as kindling for the fire. What can we do with plywood, chip-board, fibreboard, treated wood and laminates? Due to the glues, resins and waxes used in these composite boards, these should not be burned or composted. Avoiding them is not necessarily the answer either, since they make useful the waste wood bits of the timber industry. This means we get more boards per forest than we would otherwise; between plain boards and composite-wood products such as chip-board. Probably the most appropriate situation would be if the recycling sites sorted wood into natural wood suitable for chipping for landscaping purposes or fuel, and composite wood suitable for recycling into new composite board. This is already the case in Germany and the UK, facilitating the recycling of composite board products. When buying wood choose Forest Stewardship Council (FSC) certified wood, whether natural or composite. After that, make your own decisions as to whether you want to be able to use up forest waste by buying composite board, or have the capacity to use your own timber waste by buying natural wood.

- **Mixed material products** and other non-recyclables: Some products and packaging contain a combination of materials that are not easily separated. Examples include Tetra Pak and foil- or plastic-backed 'cardboard' cartons, as well as electronic equipment and wiring. The mixture of materials can make recycling difficult and potentially toxic. Tetra Pak cartons and other cardboard/metal/plastic composites are currently collected for recycling by some councils around the country. Although the cardboard is extracted for recycling into paper and the plastic is typically burned to generate heat, you don't start with another packaging carton, so more trees and plastic are needed to continue the production process. Where waste electronic equipment and wiring are exported for recycling, the component metals are sometimes reclaimed by burning off the plastic element, which can be a very hazardous and polluting process. Although neither of these examples need end up in your bin, from an ecological perspective the best option is to try and minimise mixed material products and non-recyclables that you bring into the house in the first place. Note that cardboard cartons, cardboard yoghurt cartons and similar card/plastic cartons can be deposited for collection with Tetra Paks (*not cardboard*) at recycling centres.

Products like waste electronic equipment also fall into the category of mixed material products. The recycling process can be a particularly toxic and hazardous one, especially when the plastic element of the waste is simply burned off to reclaim the metals. Get as long as possible out of your computer to minimise the volume of waste electronic equipment in the world.

Plate glass, ceramics and Pyrex are not accepted at bottle banks, but there is sometimes a container for them at recycling centres. In my experience, these do not comprise a large volume of our bin, so occasional breakages should not pose a major problem for the landfills of the country. Alternatively use under a new patio or path as fill.

Setting up the structures for reuse, rerouting and recycling

Once you have found somewhere to take your reusables and recyclables, the next step is to set up sorting and storing areas at home. To make reuse and recycling easy it is important that good structures are in place. Every house and every family will have different circumstances in terms of space, frequency of recycling runs and dedication to reducing their waste as much as possible. Each household will also have different materials for reuse and recycling, and hence different destinations. It is important that the system you adopt works for you and your family.

Before you start your waste minimisation drive, have at least:

- A shelf or box for reusable and re-routable items
- A good container for kitchen compostables
- A box for metals and glass
- A box or bag for plastics

A shelf is useful for items no longer needed, but too good for recycling. This can store items *en route* to friends, family, charity shops or repair shops. Otherwise these will continually trip you up at the front door until, in a fit of exasperation, you just fling them into the bin. That of course, would be contrary to the spirit of the endeavour.

Different recycling centres will require different levels of sorting. For maximum ease at the centre, you may wish to have a different container at home for:

- Paper
- Card
- Hard plastic
- Polythene
- Aluminium
- Glass
- Other items such as batteries, ferric metals, CDs, polystyrene etc.

Around the house you could have containers for general recyclables, to be sorted later into the different categories such as paper, plastic and card. This basically replaces the standard litter bin in the bedroom or study.

If you are keeping clean uncoloured non-glossy paper to start the fire, then this can be stored in a wastepaper basket near the source of generation – as long as everyone knows that the basket is not for plastics or glossies.

Very soon after starting your reduction measures in earnest, you will discover what recyclables need the most space and what containers are actually redundant. Change your system as often as you need to, and be imaginative about the set-up. Don't start with enormous brand new plastic boxes for each material if one cardboard box will do for glass and metals and another box for everything else. When you find out what your needs are then you can refine the set-up as you go. The last thing you want is to rush out and consume a barrel-load more of resources (and future waste products) for your waste minimisation endeavour, only to fling them out again in a month's time if they don't serve your needs.

➤ Sourcing returnables and recycled products

Returnables will only fill the shop shelves if we ask for them. Try to find returnable, refillable bottles and jars for the items that you need on a day to day basis. Sometimes the easiest way to do this is to start shopping in the country market, where every jam pot has obviously been given a new lease of life by the local preserves expert.

The availability of recycling facilities is directly dependant upon the market for the materials. If we buy more recycled paper products and stationery then the demand for waste paper will increase. If we request reusable bottles in the shops then a supplier will start supplying them in Ireland because a market will be created for them.

If we expect our waste to be collected for recycling, then we need to buy recycled products to keep the recycling industry in motion. Recycled products are also lower consumers of energy and resources than products made from virgin materials. The longest-standing supplier of 100 per cent recycled paper and stationery products in Ireland is Klee Paper in Dublin. Local health food shops often stock a range of recycled products, and your local stationery supplier may carry a range of recycled paper. The government environmental information service ENFO has information on where to source recycled paper and other recycled products. Be sure to ask for unbleached or oxygen-bleached recycled paper to minimise your environmental impact further.

GETTING RID OF YOUR BIN, ROOM BY ROOM

Now that we have examined being ruthless when shopping, composting and reusing, it is time to examine the waste sources room by room. In addition to looking at common sources of waste generation around the house, we also include work and play in order to gain the full picture of how we generate waste.

There are ideas for minimising the amount of waste produced for each activity, and sources of alternatives or further information that may be useful. Remember that this is just a list of ideas: keep your eyes, ears and mind open, and use your imagination liberally. When the whole endeavour becomes a game, then you know that you are well on your way to minimising your impact on the environment as well as the amount of money you waste.

The Kitchen – Food and Food Preparation

- Food preparation: vegetable peelings and trimmings, meat trimmings, bread and pastry crumbs
- Cooking: grill pan fat, deep-fryer fat
- Packaging: cans, tins, plastic wrapping
- Leftovers

- Food storage: freezing, dry, fridge, shelving, spoiling, preserving
- Shopping: where it all starts
- Diet: what you put in your shopping basket, what you put in you
- Wastewater and energy issues in the kitchen
- Social and ethical issues beyond the kitchen

Food preparation: vegetable peelings and trimmings, meat trimmings, bread and pastry crumbs

Compost vegetable trimmings; feed meat trimmings to pets; put bread and pastry crumbs on the bird table. Clean vegetable peelings and trimmings can be made into vegetable stock, or frozen until there is a sufficient quantity to do so.

Cooking: grill pan fat, deep-fryer fat

Use grill-pan fat in newspaper as firelighters, minimise deep-fryer use and return oil to council bring site or find a friend with a converted diesel engine that is suitable for using vegetable oil. Let children make bird feeders: pour melted fat into egg cartons full of nuts and seeds, and then hang upside down from the bird table when solid.

Packaging: cans, tins, plastic wrapping

Minimise what packaging enters the house; wash all cans and tins and put with food cans or scrap metals container in council bring sites as appropriate. When shopping give priority to dried beans rather than canned and to fresh fish rather than tinned. Separate paper from cans and send each to recycling. Wash plastic wrapping before recycling to avoid attracting rodents to the recycling centre and to avoid a whole container load of plastic being dumped by the collection company.

Leftovers

To avoid leftovers, try not to cook too much for you to eat. Keep any leftovers still in the pan or dish, rather than dumping – either freeze or refrigerate, and reuse at a later meal; feed meat scraps to pets; compost vegetable scraps in a rodent-proof compost system; put suitable leftovers such as bread, crackers, pulses etc. on the bird table, or keep hens ... It is sometimes recommended to clear the bird table at night into a good compost system, to avoid encouraging rodents – but a good tall table will also work. Try to scrape pans really clean before washing, instead of having food washed down the sink contribute to water pollution.

Food storage: freezing, dry, fridge, shelving, spoiling, preserving

Proper storage prevents spoilage and wastage of food. It should be unnecessary to buy freezer bags, since enough suitable bags usually come in with the shopping around things like cornflakes, bread, dried beans etc. Large yoghurt cartons and Tetra Pak cartons make good freezer boxes for soups, stews and stock and can be easily torn away for reheating, or melted off with warm water and used again. Buying in bulk can help to reduce the amount of packaging consumed, but also remember that the less you store the fewer storage containers and less storage space you need. If you preserve your own food you can reuse old jars and bottles as well as cutting down on costs and waste. Where food is stored on shelves, ensure that it is reasonably cool and out of direct sunlight to avoid spoiling.

Shopping: where it all starts

Avoid packaging like the plague. Choose loose fruit and vegetables; choose raw ingredients rather than heavily-packaged ready meals; choose packaging materials that are easily recyclable or have a low embodied energy. Use cotton, jute or hemp bags rather than plastic or synthetic ones so that you can compost the bag when it finally needs to be sent on its way. As an experiment, try cutting packaging out completely for a week.

Diet: what you put in your shopping basket, what you put in you

How does diet fit into a waste minimisation plan? Generally a reduction in packaging coincides with a reduction in highly-processed foods, which are also generally high in salt, sugar, fat and additives. An organic, wholefood diet is both good for the environment and for your health, and usually has less, or more easily recycled, packaging.

Wastewater and energy issues in the kitchen

Think beyond the bin and consider energy use and wastewater, particularly in the kitchen. Allow all food to cool before refrigerating or freezing, to minimise wasting energy. Do not install a garbage grinder because it increases the wastewater pollution load leaving the house. Use a spatula on saucepans to make sure all food waste is removed for the same reason. Take care not to leave taps running and to fix any leaky ones that drip. A surprising volume of water can be wasted one drip at a time. How you cook also has a direct bearing on energy use. For example proper soaking of rice and pulses cuts down cooking time, and for real enthusiasts hay-box cookers can be used to slow-cook pot stews for dinner after just an initial heat in the morning.

Social and ethical issues beyond the kitchen

Although not a waste issue exactly, consider the wider implications of your shopping choices. Imported items like chocolate, tea and coffee are often produced by growers who are paid a pittance and who often have to put up with unhealthy work conditions. Look for Fairtrade chocolate, tea and coffee to guarantee that your money is supporting ethical producers. Many Irish towns and cities are now Fairtrade towns, expanding the range of choice available to the conscientious shopper. When shopping use your LOAF (Local, Organic, Animal-friendly, Fairtrade) as a reminder.

The Kitchen – Washing and Cleaning

- Cleaning products
- Packaging
- Wastewater considerations

Cleaning products

Cleaning products such as soap, washing-up liquid, dish-washer detergent, scouring powder, window cleaner etc. can all be substituted with safer, less environmentally impacting and less waste-generating products. Bread soda makes a very good scouring powder; environmentally friendly soap, washing-up liquid and dishwasher detergent are available in good health food shops. A mixture of hot water and vinegar makes a good window cleaner and general degreaser, while a couple of drops of tea-tree oil can be used as an antibacterial, antifungal ingredient in wash-water where necessary. Use washable dish- and floor-cloths instead of paper towels, preferably made from well-worn cotton clothing that isn't good enough for the charity shop. Old T-shirts are excellent.

Many of the standard cleaning products that we use around the home are, in fact, quite harmful for us. They can enter the body via the skin when we are washing and cleaning, and can remain on our eating utensils to be ingested. By using vinegar, tea-tree oil, bread soda and hot water in various combinations we can get the house spick and span without using anything harmful in the process. These are all available either in a local grocer or good health food shop.

Packaging

Packaging should be kept to a minimum at all times. Eco-friendly cleaning products are generally not grossly over-packaged, but whatever choice you make, try to find packaging materials that you can readily recycle locally. Always look for single-material packaging or packaging that can be easily separated for recycling. Concentrated products can cut down on packaging, but be sure to use only the right amount, or less, to avoid putting excess down the drain. Some health food shops offer a refill service for washing machine detergent and washing-up liquid, which is direct reuse rather than recycling and thus much more sustainable.

Wastewater considerations

Every cleaner or chemical that you use in your sink or on surfaces around the house ultimately goes down the drain. Whether you live in the town and send all your water to a council treatment plant and then to the river, or live in the countryside and have a septic tank feeding to the groundwater, these chemicals ultimately end up in the local environment.

Cleaning chemicals can have toxic and harmful elements such as heavy metals, which are not removed in sewage treatment, but remain in the water or the sludge and can accumulate in the environment. It therefore makes sense that if you use food products such as vinegar and bread soda to clean, this has less impact on your groundwater than chemical cleaners. If you must use whatever it is that you 'can't live without', try to minimise it. At the very least, using just a dash rather than a good squirt will cut your chemical usage, your bills and your waste packaging.

The Bathroom

- Shampoos and soap
- Cleaning products
- Cosmetics
- Washing machine
- Toilet paper and sanitary items

Shampoos and soap

Check that you do not use more shampoo or soap than is necessary. To minimise embodied waste – waste created during the manufacturing process – source products that have returnable packaging and products that have only natural materials. Use soap bars rather than liquid soaps to cut down on packaging, or better still buy unwrapped, natural soap.

Cleaning products

Substitute bread soda for scouring powder and use vinegar as a degreaser. Tea-tree oil makes a good antibacterial agent. Chlorine bleach kills off essential septic tank bacteria, so rule that out completely. Natural citrus-based toilet cleaners can be used instead of conventional products. Try Irish-made Lilly's Eco-clean cleaning products for an eco-friendly alternative to the usual cleaners and detergents.

Cosmetics

Do you need cosmetics? If you want them, source those that are as natural as possible to minimise embodied waste and animal testing. Try to take only packaging that is easily recyclable or reusable where possible.

Washing machine

There are many environmentally-friendly washing powders or liquids available. Some laundry magnets/balls/discs work well as an alternative to washing powder, or at least as a way to minimise powder use. As with shampoos, soaps, cleaning products and cosmetics, good health food shops will stock washing powders or liquids that are less environmentally damaging than conventional alternatives.

Toilet paper and sanitary items

Recycled paper toilet tissue is readily available and less grossly wasteful than felling forests and chlorine bleaching! Sanitary products are available in recycled, unbleached paper. Washable organic cotton sanitary products are also available in good health food shops and via the internet from Irish suppliers (see the appendices for details).

The Bedroom

- Clothes and bed linen
- Footwear
- Storage

Clothes and bed linen

Buy only what you need, rather than engaging in systematic impulse buying. If you stick to classic styles, the changes in trends and fashions will 'date' your clothes less. Buy natural fibres for preference, because these can be composted when they are completely worn through. Organic clothing has the added advantage of minimising embodied waste and environmental damage from spraying operations. Cotton is usually a very spray-intensive crop, so investigate bamboo, soya or hemp clothing as an ecological alternative.

Buying Irish clothing cuts out much of the energy used in transportation, assuming that the raw materials needed to be transported to the factory anyway. Bring unwanted clothes to second-hand shops to minimise waste and to allow good clothing to continue to be used. Buy what you can at second-hand shops also, to minimise packaging and embodied waste in new clothes production, and to keep your clothing spend as close to carbon neutral as possible. Natural and synthetic fabrics can be brought to textile bring-banks. Buying good quality, long-lasting clothing will maximise the life that you get from your clothes. Natural hemp clothing and organic cotton clothing are available in growing numbers of shops in Ireland or can be purchased by internet and mail order.

Footwear

Shoes, boots, wellies, sandals, clogs, overshoes, waders,

flippers, roller-blades … Whatever you have on your feet, just use it carefully, care for it, and use it out! Generally the more natural the process (real leather, rubber or cork) the less the embodied waste involved. Send good but unwanted footwear to second-hand shops.

Storage

Storage is often a problem area in many houses. It may not seem like a waste issue *per se*, but just think of the amount of waste generated by building an extension, for example. Most extensions are built because 'there isn't enough space for everything'. An immediate way to cut down on storage requirements is to minimise the amount of clothing (and other 'stuff') that you have. Check what you actually *use*, and keep that, but send the rest off to a charity shop so that somebody else can get use out it other than the moths.

The Living-room

- Games
- TV
- Reading material
- Music

Games

Think versatility when buying children's games and toys – e.g. cards or a football vs single-application games, which may also be bulky and/or battery-operated. Remember that natural materials have maximum recycling potential. Avoid rushing out to buy the 'next big thing' if you think that it will not last the pace. There are as many trends in toys as in clothes. Beware of them, because they come and go and leave 'stuff' clogging up your house afterwards. Avoid toys with batteries to minimise this hazardous waste source. Old toys can be given to charity shops if they are in good order, or sold via LETS (Local Exchange Trading Systems) or car-boot sales. Make full use of available materials, particularly for young children who need constant entertainment and new stimulation. Cardboard tubes, wooden spoons, saucepan lids, pebbles and other everyday objects make fascinating playthings for toddlers and young children. Washing up at the kitchen sink with dad or mum may be much more fun than playing alone with a mini plastic kitchen.

TV

Television is a disaster for waste minimisation. There is no other medium through which the message of 'buy more stuff' comes with more force than TV. To be attractive: buy. To be popular: buy. To be sexy: buy. To be intelligent: buy. Whatever your imagined character flaw happens to be (and comparisons with the rich, famous and made-over are a sure way to find it) if you buy something then you will be OK – until the next ad, soap or film comes on. Suggestion No. 1: dump your TV. Dump it, or give it away to a friend (or enemy if you have one) or a charity shop or anywhere, but get it out of your house. If that is a bit extreme for you, just drastically reduce the amount of time you spend in front of it, and be very selective about what you and your children watch.

The average time spent watching TV in Ireland is twenty-three hours per week, fourth on the world list after the US, the UK and Italy. That is a lot of ads telling us and our children what to think, what to do, what to say, what to eat and most importantly from a waste point of view, what to buy. Lots! is the constant mantra. We haven't even mentioned DVDs, videos, computer games etc. The mainstream media urges greater consumption, even if it is the Discovery Channel showing beautiful people swimming over coral reefs. The ad there is flights, hotels and diving trips. From a waste perspective: minimise as always.

Reading material

Newspapers are readily recyclable, can be soaked in water, covered in grass clippings and used as mulch around young trees, can make papier mâché for children (or adults) or can be used to light the fire in the mornings. However, it still takes energy and resources to produce and transport the paper in the first place. How many do you buy? Can you cut that down?

Glossy magazines are not suitable for garden mulch or papier mâché and should not be burned. They do recycle, which cuts down your bin charges, but recycling paper takes energy too, so minimise your purchasing if possible. Most environmental magazines now come on recycled, unbleached paper: look for these in preference to virgin, chlorine-bleached paper. Environmentally-focused publications are also more likely to confirm the ideals of waste reduction rather than the opposite.

For books, the library is an invaluable resource. Not only is the existing stock of books at your disposal, but you can order new books too. Most second-hand shops will do a part-exchange on returned titles. For novels and books that you may not want to read a second time these are excellent ways to keep them off your shelves and out of your bin – not that there is much chance of them being dumped, with charity shops and second-hand book shops ready to take them.

Music

Music can produce waste in the form of LPs, tapes, CDs and old stereo equipment. Make your own music if you have instruments, or sing. Children in particular love this interaction. Listen to the radio or try your library rather than buying more CDs. Make full use of the music you have before buying more. Appreciate what you already have and buy carefully if you do want more music around. Take good care of your musical equipment and instruments, so that they will last a lifetime.

Lighting and Heating

- Light fittings and bulbs
- Heating systems
- Fireplaces

Light fittings and bulbs

Compact fluorescent lamps (CFLs) last longer than ordinary tungsten bulbs and have a lower energy usage. However they are fluorescent tubes and contain mercury, so they need to be brought to a hazardous waste collection point, or usually your local recycling centre, after they are finished with. LED bulbs are being developed and marketed which use less energy again and last longer. These are mainly available in the US, but check the shops or the internet occasionally for Irish-compatible models. Use CFLs and LEDs where possible to replace all standard bulbs in the home.

Heating systems

Heating systems come in all shapes and sizes; fuelled by oil, gas, solid fuel (wood, coal, peat), electric, solar, or a combination of these. Oil, gas and electricity are all low producers of on-site waste. However, they are all fossil energy and thus use up scarce, non-renewable resources and should be avoided where possible. Coal is also a fossil fuel and has the further waste-related disadvantage of having coal bags and coal ash to dispose of afterwards. Peat, another fossil fuel, comes from our beautifully diverse peatland habitat, a valuable carbon sink, and should be avoided too.

That leaves wood, which can be ordered by the trailer load if you have somewhere to store it and can be replanted as soon as it is cut, ready to harvest again in less than a generation. Ashes from wood (and peat) can be used around trees in small amounts as a mulch and fertiliser. Coal ash is not recommended in the garden, so burn something else if your concern is minimising your bin weight. Do not burn plastic in the fire since many plastics are toxic when burned. That includes envelopes with windows, plastic tape on boxes, plastic in floor sweepings, fire-lighter bags, peat briquette straps and anything else that may be tempted to cross the hearth. Avoid the plastic to protect the environment as well as the health of you and your neighbours.

Solar heat is readily available and should be harnessed where possible. South-facing glass, solar panels and careful house designs are all good ways to maximise the use of this abundant energy supply. Houses can now be built to 'passive standard', requiring almost no external heat sources after the sun, cooking and body heat are considered.

Pellet stoves, wood chip boilers, log gasifiers, geo-thermal heating and solar panels are all increasing in diversity and efficiency each year. For an in-depth look at home heating investigate these options thoroughly. PV (photo voltaic) cells are sometimes connected to an immersion to convert the excess electricity into hot water directly rather than feeding it back to the grid or to batteries.

Fireplaces

Stoves are much more efficient than open fireplaces and can easily be retrofitted. If you are at the design stage for your house, investigate masonry (ceramic) stoves for maximising fuel burn efficiency and minimising fuel use. *The Green Building Bible* has a chapter on wood burning. *The Earth Care Manual* has a section on heating with wood, including a description of masonry stoves, as has John Seymour's *Complete Book of Self-Sufficiency*. These books are listed in the appendices. From a waste perspective, the more efficient your heating system is, the less ash will be produced in the year, and the less effort and resources are devoted to providing the wood fuel. If you are using wood, the ash can be used to enrich your fruit trees and shrubs.

Furnishing

- Fitted furniture
- Free-standing furniture
- Floor coverings
- White goods

Fitted furniture

Fitted furniture is generally less versatile than free-standing. However if you are putting it in, design it for maximum reuse elsewhere so that it can be moved to another room, a new house, sold, or given away, rather than dumped. Otherwise try to reuse the materials instead of dumping them. If you use natural untreated wood rather than wood composites, painted or preserved wood, then the timber can be safely used as firewood later, if no other use can be found for it.

Free-standing furniture

For other furniture minimise chemical inputs and maximise the use it gets, either in your own home or in somebody else's. Buy and Sell, local free-ad newspapers and Freecycle are wonderful vehicles for sending on old furniture to new homes. Consider an Irish made native hardwood item instead of tropical hardwood or pine. These can often be found in small specialist furniture shops. Remember that second-hand items are carbon and resource neutral.

Floor coverings

For floor coverings remember that ceramic tiles, quarry tiles, stone, cork tiles, lino (PVC), carpets, underlay, rugs, paints, varnishes, sealants, waxes, and other finishes all have different energy inputs, waste outputs and lifetimes. Maximise your product lifetime while minimising the chemical inputs and keeping reuse or safe disposal in mind. For minimum waste generation in the long term consider stone, quarry tile or timber that will have a good resale value when it is removed if the house is being renovated or demolished. If disposing of existing floor coverings: carpet tiles are very transportable and carpets can sometimes be reused or passed on to a suitable home (e.g. a local charity or to St Vincent de Paul), or used to cover vegetable beds as a weed suppressor. *The Green Building Bible* has information and listings on environmentally-friendly floor coverings for new projects.

White goods

If you are buying a new fridge or washing machine, buy the most energy-efficient and water-efficient model that is available within your budget. This will minimise your energy consumption and the related waste involved in electricity production. Before buying, however, be sure that the purchase is necessary. An old model can be more efficient than a new one if you count in manufacture and transport energy and waste. Old fridges and freezers need to be taken to the local landfill site or recycling centre for refrigerant gas recovery. Do not forget second-hand shops or the St Vincent de Paul society if you are getting rid of an old but functioning appliance.

Children

- Babies
- Older children
- Teens

Babies: nappies, creams, shampoos, clothes

Nappies are the waste mentioned over and over again by parents wishing to reduce their bin weight. The easy solution: use cloth nappies. These are available now in fitted shapes with Velcro fasteners, comfy waterproof covers and paper inserts. The inserts were the thing that won me over – just lift up the contents and flush down the loo! Recycled paper disposable nappies are available in good health food shops, as are Calendula cream in glass jars or metal tubes and shampoos in recyclable containers. Charity shops and friends are great for babies' clothes because they grow out of them so quickly. Once your own children are finished with them you can then give the clothes away to be reused again.

Older children: entertainment, clothes

Entertain without battery-operated toys where possible. Maximise the amount of time you spend with your children, rather than the amount of money spent buying 'stuff' for them. Use charity shops, second-hand shops and Buy and Sell to both get, and get rid of, toys and clothes. We have a general rule that says: 'OK, if you can find a bag of things for the charity shop, you can buy something there to replace it', thus getting the children's de-cluttering muscles going.

Teens: entertainment, clothes, make-up?

As children get older, the same ideas apply. Again, maximise time input over stuff input. Let them see the waste issue in terms of what they buy and how its disposal has to be paid for if it cannot be used elsewhere or avoided in the first place. As for make-up; as children grow into adults, they will experiment with styles and with their way of presenting themselves to the world. Don't let waste minimisation become an obstacle to good relationships – that would be a waste indeed. You can encourage them to go for the options listed under 'cosmetics' in the section on bathrooms.

Parties

- Birthdays
- Weddings, funerals, christenings
- Christmas, Easter, Hallowe'en

Birthdays

Keep parties activity-centred, rather than stuff-centred. If you minimise the unhealthy stuff – the crisps, sweets, chocolates, biscuits etc. – you will generally cut down on much of the plastic wrapping too. Health, wallet and environment go together here: home-baked savoury party foods are enjoyed every bit as much as sugar-stuffed plastic-packaged sweets and snacks. Gifts are also an issue. Exercise your imagination to source gifts that will be appreciated, but that don't cost the earth. Any number of environmental/conservation charities and eco-shops have sprung up over the last decade offering great gift ideas with minimum ecological impact. If there are none in your area, check the internet for mail-order eco-shopping.

Weddings, funerals, christenings

Weddings, funerals and christenings are all times when huge pressure can be brought to bear on people to have the latest trend, or to follow tradition rather than personal preference or common sense. Use these occasions to put all the other lifestyle changes into practice. At gatherings of any sort avoid using disposable cups, plates and cutlery. Friends often weigh in on such occasions with offers of salads and dishes of different sorts; enjoy the communal element of these rather than dashing out to buy prepared packaged meals. Consider a cardboard coffin for yourself if you want to make that final eco-gesture.

Christmas, Easter, Hallowe'en
Are these festivals a childhood dream or a waste minimisation nightmare? It is possible to celebrate the year without enormous waste generation, but it takes a lot of thought, commitment and imagination and oodles of tact. It is difficult to control what actually comes into the house at these times without causing offence to in-laws and out-laws, the Easter Bunny, neighbours and friends. However, you can ensure that the presents you give contain loving intent rather than unnecessary junk bulked up with pretty packaging. As an example, the advent of charity donation cards opens the way for giving goodwill rather than 'stuff', in a way that actively helps those who need it. Easter can be a time for making chocolate eggs, at home, rather than being forced to buy the packaging that comes with commercial eggs. Try to take home less packaging when shopping, and recycle all the plastic, card and/or foil that come with the shop-bought eggs. Hallowe'en is traditionally associated with nuts, dried fruits and apples, all of which have low waste implications.

Gardens, Sheds, Pets, Cars/Bicycles
- Trimmings/prunings/mowings
- Garden furniture

- Hard landscaping
- Soft landscaping
- Garden machinery
- Packaging
- Shed storage
- Pets
- Cars/Bicycles

Trimmings/prunings/mowings

Don't dream of dumping your garden trimmings, prunings and mowings and the nutrient value that is in them: make compost! For bigger branches, cut them and dry them for firewood.

Garden furniture

Make your own garden furniture from old timber, stone or brick. Alternatively buy timber furniture that can be used as firewood when it reaches the end of its life, avoid preservatives and treated wood. Care for outdoor furniture appropriately to lengthen its lifespan. Over-wintering it in the garden shed is one way to help it live longer without chemicals.

Hard landscaping

When designing hard landscaping, maximise the use of naturally-available stone, timber etc. in preference to materials which will need to be disposed of when the landscaping changes. Keep it simple. Use materials already on-site where possible.

Soft landscaping

Growing plants from cuttings and seed is less pack-aging intensive and costly than lots of pot-grown plants. Friends' gardens are often abundantly planted with raw materials for cuttings. Swap, for twice the minimisation. Again, keep it simple. Avoid peat moss to save the bogs – you will have plenty of home-made compost. If you really cannot get to making it yourself, coconut fibre or Gee-up composted horse manure are good alternatives to peat moss, certainly from the frog's perspective. How-ever, if you have read this far, then composting should be a breeze.

Garden machinery

Garden machinery such as mowers, electric clippers, strimmers and the like, all take up a lot more space than the manual alternative. To minimise the space they take up in your bin at the end of their lives, avoid buying them as a first step. Otherwise keep them well maintained so that they last as long as possible. Is it just my imagination or does older equipment tend to outlast newer models fairly consistently? The moral: keep your mower and just get it serviced rather than replaced. Alternatively adopt a permaculture garden design and grow a forest garden where your lawn was: no mowing, less watering, visually attractive and lots of fresh fruit and nuts in the harvest season. Read the *Earth Care Manual* listed in the appendix for in-depth information on forest gardening and permaculture.

Packaging of plants and paraphernalia

Reuse pots or send them in to your local school garden project. Minimise the packaging you buy. Instead of endless plastic/card/foil seed packets, consider saving your own seed. Alternatively buy them in plain polythene sachets which can be reused or recycled or in paper envelopes which can be reused, recycled, composted or burned (available from the Irish Seed Saver Association or the appropriately named Brown Envelope Seeds).

Shed storage

When it comes to storage, minimise your junk: that will minimise the storage space you need. Sheds are great for holding lots of stuff and are a lot less resource hungry than a house extension, but if you send unwanted stuff off for appropriate reuse or recycling then a smaller shed will do. Moving things along also keeps them in use, minimising everybody's consumption of new, resource-intensive things.

Pets

Feed pets on meat scraps as well as any other food they may need – make friends with a local restaurant and get good meat scraps from them rather than heavily pack-aged pet food. Use your common sense with this, and avoid small bones or overly fatty meat if you want to keep your pets healthy. Keep hens rather than budgies as a way to use kitchen scraps and to minimise egg pack-aging! Clearly this is easier in large gardens, but I have friends who keep hens very successfully in a small town garden.

Cars/Bicycles

The car is a relatively invisible contributor to waste because it doesn't end up in your weekly bin. However the resources used to scrap and rebuild cars are vast, before ever you count in maintenance of the roads and services needed to run a car. So if you use one, keep it well maintained and hang onto it as long as you can. The resources required to maintain an old car are far, far lower than those required to produce a new one.

Where practical, walk, cycle or take the bus or train rather than drive. Telecommute rather than sit in traffic. As a waste issue on the train, a packed lunch will have less plastic than a wrapped muffin and a disposable coffee cup.

Keeping more of your journeys within walking and cycling distance is the best transport option of all. It is healthier by far as well as costing less. In waste terms, sell your old bike or give it away to an overseas, or local, charity if you really want a new one, rather than paying to have it dumped. Use your bike regularly to keep it (and you) fit. Keep it well maintained to prevent it rusting away. Buy and Sell lists second-hand cars and bikes, which is much more environmentally friendly than buying new. At the end of the day, an old bike is much less bulky to dump than an old car!

DIY/Construction

- Wood and wood products
- Aggregates and blocks
- Cement, plasters and admixtures
- Adhesives, fillers, fittings
- Finishes
- Tools

Wood: untreated, treated, composite (plywood, fibre-board, chipboard, laminates)

Natural untreated wood is the best option from a house-hold waste minimisation perspective, because it can be used as kindling after all of its other uses have been explored. Do not burn composite boards because of the air pollution generated by the glues and resins. Larger recycling centres usually have a depot for waste wood. Ask what happens to the wood you bring to the centre. Recycling composite board back into chip-board is a more ecologically sound option than adding the glues and resins to the air by burning or to the soil by chipping for landscaping.

Aggregates: gravel, sand, stone, left-over blocks

Sand and gravel do not have a large waste footprint, but minimise as always on energy and environmental grounds. Leftover sand can be used for children's sand pits. Recycled demolition aggregates are increasingly used to generate aggregates for road construction while minimising the use of landfill space. Builders' rubble can be used as driveway fill for easy on-site recycling of clean demolition wastes.

Cement, plasters and admixtures: lime, skim-coat, bonding, rapid hardener, plasticiser

Keep different types of wastes separate so that each material can be evaluated for recycling on its own. Keep materials covered and appropriately stored so that they do not spoil. This maximises the percentage that can be used on site, on other jobs, returned or recycled. Use materials within their expiry date rather than storing until they need to be dumped. Make sure all powdered products are kept airtight during storage, and ideally used as soon after opening as possible.

Adhesives, fillers, fittings: wood glue, painters mate, silicone, plaster and all purpose adhesives, nails, screws

For adhesives and related products, as always, avoid mixing. These are not easy materials to deal with, often containing toxic or hazardous elements, so minimise their use and buy only in the volumes that you need. *The Green Building Bible* offers environmentally friendly alternatives to many of these products. Obviously nails, screws and fittings can be extracted carefully for reuse, or recycled for their metal if damaged.

Finishes: tile, panel board, paint, wallpaper, varnishes, timber floor boards, composite floor boards, vinyl

When it comes to finishes, usually the more environmentally friendly options will have wastes that are easier to deal with than the standard products. For example it is safe to burn untreated waste timber, but toxic to burn waste lino/vinyl (PVC). High-quality leftover materials can be reused on other construction jobs: timber, roofing materials, piping, plastics, aggregates, cement and admixtures, insulation materials, nails, screws, electrical and plumbing fittings and blocks. 'As new' leftover materials can sometimes be returned to the suppliers, cutting down on costs, waste generation and clutter. Otherwise set up a swap site in your neighbourhood to get full use out of materials that are not needed for a job. Cardboard and plastics are often used as packing materials for deliveries to construction sites and new houses and can be recycled if they are kept clean. Burning rubbish on site is illegal and can be harmful to your health if plastics, composite wood products, paint or glues are included.

Tools: carpenter's kit, plasterer's kit, block work tools, tiler's kit, painters kit

Paints, varnishes, wood stains, preservatives, adhesives and other products and materials can be kept and used on other jobs. Sometimes there are paint collection points for community groups to utilise leftover paint, or list it on your local Freecycle.org list. These are good ways to ensure that leftover paint and other surplus materials are used. Waste generated by electricians and plumbers is generally clean and readily recyclable. Electric wiring needs to be separated into copper and plastic before recycling, the copper because of the potential for dioxin generation.

For tools themselves, keep them in good condition to maximise their lifespan. Pass them on if you won't use them again, so you don't clog up your storage space.

The ultimate waste minimisation measure in DIY is 'don't build'. A few years ago we decided *not* to extend! The decision has reduced our waste, our resource consumption, our heating bills, our 'space-to-be-filled-with-stuff', our financial outgoings and the stress of doing the job. Instead we took a long hard look at all of the possessions and material we had accumulated and managed to send a lot of it to charities, friends, recycling and bookshops. Another vital component is to stop bringing stuff into the house – to simplify. Now we have a spare room again, instead of being a room short!

Toxic and hazardous components can be present in insulation materials, wood preservatives, propellants for spray applications, glues, admixtures, varnishes, paints and other commonly used builders' materials. Appropriate disposal of such wastes is necessary. Contact an ecological shop or green building supplier for more information on the most sustainable building materials available.

The Office

- Paper and stationery
- Incoming post

- Storage facilities
- Computer/photocopier/printer/phone

Paper and stationery

Whether your business is consultancy, farming, account-ing or bird-watching: office work of some sort is usually a necessity. Use both sides of all paper. Use the reverse side of all suitable 'waste' paper for printing your own records and accounts. Pencils use fewer resources than pens and contribute less to landfill when they are finished with. Klee Paper and others supply recycled stationery: why not maximise the availability of recycling facilities by supporting the sale of recycled products?

Incoming post

All incoming post constitutes potential waste or potential resources, depending on how you look at it. Many envelopes are now self-adhesive and can be opened carefully for reuse. A sticker can be stuck on over the old address to save on paper and costs, or envelope reuse labels can be bought from your favourite charity. It is a double bonus to reuse envelopes with windows because they are difficult to recycle due to the paper and plastic being glued together, and it can negate the need for a sticker if done carefully. All coloured or glossy paper should be sent for recycling rather than fire-lighting. If junk mail is a particular problem, look for the small print on the mailing that shows the originator of the mail list, phone the number given and request to have your details removed. To head off unaddressed junk mail, An Post suggests a 'No Junk Mail' sticker on your letterbox.

Storage facilities

Storage space is a constant issue in offices. De-clutter as much as possible and cut down on what you choose to store. Remember that every storage system, whether it is shelving, filing cabinets or box files, will need to be disposed of after the end of its useful life. Plan for durability and ideally for future separation for reuse or recycling at the end of the product life. Buy recycled cardboard folders, binders, box files etc. These are much easier to dispose of than their plastic equivalents.

Computer/photocopier/printer/phone

Electronic items are typically large and bulky and are increasingly illegal to dispose of via the normal bin collection. Where computers, printers, copiers etc. are necessary, plan for durability. The longer you get out of your computer the higher the spec of the next one. Get things fixed where possible, rather than buying new ones. If you can postpone changing your printer for as long as possible, you keep it out of landfill or incineration, avoid the disposal cost and avoid the cost of a new one. For me the difference between a 'friendly old printer' and a 'frustrating wreck on its last legs' was a judiciously-placed piece of card taped to the paper feed tray to keep it going smoothly! (Sellotape is a cellulose product and as such is more environmentally friendly than plastic sticky tape.) Printer cartridge refills and recycling facilities are available. Ask at your usual stationery supplier or find a local charity that collects them to raise funds.

WASTE MINIMISATION REMINDERS

The following waste minimisation tips have been picked from various government and county council websites, with a few changes and additions. They are included here as reminders and pointers for the journey towards getting rid of your bin completely.

- Always carry a reusable bag when shopping – don't accept every paper bag you are offered.
- Avoid disposable products, such as disposable nappies, tissues, face wipes, razors, paper and plastic cups, plates and cutlery, kitchen towels, serviettes and disposable cameras.
- Bring a lunchbox to school/work and use a box with a lid at home instead of using foil or cling film.
- Bring all your household batteries to the collection points at the local recycling centre. Alternatively new legislation requires any retailer that sells batteries to accept old ones of a similar type for appropriate disposal, whether you are purchasing a new battery or not.
- Bring old glasses back to the optician for use in the developing world, or use your existing frames if all you need is new lenses.

- Buy in bulk where possible, to minimise packaging.
- Choose products in returnable containers whenever possible.
- Buy unpackaged goods and avoid over-packaged products, choosing loose fruit and vegetables instead of pre-packed ones.
- Compost organic waste from your kitchen and garden.
- Donate books, clothes and toys to charity shops and jumble sales. Otherwise sell via second-hand shops, Buy and Sell or eBay.
- Drink tap water instead of bottled water.
- Finish off jars of food, tubes of toothpaste and bottles of lotion fully before opening new ones.
- Give preference to products made from recycled materials.
- Join your local library.
- Leave newspaper supplements you are not going to read in the shop.
- Many pharmacies will accept unused medicines.
- Only buy what you need: the more you buy, the more you'll throw out!
- Pass on unwanted clothes, mobile phones and furniture to friends, charities and second-hand shops.
- Print draft quality where appropriate to save on ink.
- Purchase refillable containers for cleaners, washing solutions and detergents whenever possible.
- Recycle ink jet/toner cartridges and mobile phones through your supplier.

- Repair electrical appliances rather than replacing them if at all possible.
- Return junk mail to sender and have your name removed from the mailing list.
- Reuse envelopes; purchase reuse labels or print your own.
- Send emails instead of paper memos whenever possible (and don't print your emails).
- Share magazines with friends and see if your GP or dentist can use unwanted magazines in the waiting-room.
- Tick boxes in surveys stating no requirement for further unsolicited mail-shot material.
- Use a battery recharger and use rechargeable batteries.
- Use a vacuum cleaner with reusable/washable bags, or better still, use a sweeping brush.
- Use and refill your own drinks bottle (with water!) rather than buying new.
- Use broken crockery as drainage in plant pots.
- Use glass instead of plastic where possible.
- Buy items that will last and are durable.
- Use old clothes as rags if they are beyond wearing.
- When using paper – use both sides of the page. Keep single-sided scrap paper for reusing and printing drafts.

A BIT MORE DETAIL

Hidden Waste – Food Miles, Product Miles, Embodied Energy and Embodied Waste

Food miles could be defined as 'The total distance travelled to get food from the field to the table, including the miles travelled by each ingredient in each product or dish.' I have seen an estimate from Germany for a pot of yoghurt having a total of 700 food miles. Presumably this included the local milk products used, imported strawberries, imported sugar, starter cultures, travel to the wholesaler, travel to the retailer and finally delivery to the table.

Clearly from an environmental point of view, the lower the food miles, the lower the environmental impact. The less food miles a product travels the less energy, oil and resources are consumed in getting it from field to table.

When we extend the principle of food miles to 'product miles', we become more aware of every purchase. The important questions become:

- Where does a product come from? The closer the better.
- Where do the raw materials come from? The closer to the site of production the better.

- How many different raw materials and sources are used? The fewer the better, usually.

The impacts of the energy consumption of food miles and product miles are many, and are examined below under the heading of 'embodied energy'. The waste implications of both food miles and product miles are principally derived from transportation and associated packaging. These are waste sources that do not show up in your weekly bin, but still contribute to our national and international waste mountains.

The transport options

Road – One estimate that I glanced at years ago suggested that lorries exert about one million times more wear on roads than cars, principally a function of the weight of the vehicles involved. The figure may be way off the mark, but it serves to highlight a general point: the more road freight that moves around, the more our roads need upkeep and maintenance, and the more energy used and waste generated in the process. The general move towards ever more and bigger supermarkets has led to ever greater road haulage, as our supermarket warehouses are now effectively the rolling stock on our roads.

Air – Air travel consumes vast quantities of fuel and as such is very wasteful of energy. Surely it is not worth risking the very health of our planet to import cut flowers by air when we can grow our own using just a fraction of the energy, for example.

Sea – Water transport is one of the more energy-efficient means of transporting goods, although there are also dangers associated with this. Spilled cargo can be polluting, e.g. spillages of oil or raw materials can be damaging to wildlife. Even spillages of relatively innocuous products such as plastic pellets can be fatal to birds when mistaken for food.

Local production – This is an obvious solution, and works admirably for many items. Local food production is already enjoying an upsurge in popularity with farmers' markets and the international Slow Food movement.

In addition to the energy implications of travel, copious amounts of packaging are required to transport items safely. Much of the packaging used for transporting products from A to B would not be necessary if the source and end use were closer together. The volume of plastic and cardboard dumped by retailers is vast, before the product is even placed in the shopping basket.

In short, product miles contribute substantially to both embodied energy and embodied waste. Buy local or grow your own to keep your product miles and food miles to a minimum.

Embodied energy

Embodied energy is the energy that is used in the manufacture of a product, including the transportation of raw materials, packaging and the finished item itself. The lower the embodied energy, the smaller our carbon footprint – the amount of carbon dioxide we produce through energy consumption by all our travel, purchases, and lifestyle choices. For example in building our homes, products like concrete blocks have a much greater embodied energy than timber, because the manufacture of cement consumes huge amounts of power.

The waste implications of embodied energy include the wastes generated by the oil industry and other fossil fuel industries as well as electricity generation and energy transport via cables, trucks or oil tankers. The higher the embodied energy of a product, the greater the waste generated by some or all of these industries. Like other hidden wastes, this cost is not borne directly at the weekly bin, but in product costs, taxes and tertiary costs associated with environmental change. Well-known western-world examples of the cost of environmental change include the social and economic costs of Hurricane Katrina in New Orleans and bushfires in Australia, and the loss of tens of thousands of lives in the heat waves here in Europe. Although we do not always hear as much about them, climate-related disasters are also being exacerbated on a grand scale in Asia, Africa and South America.

Embodied waste

Embodied waste is the waste trail left by the products we buy. Embodied waste is similar to embodied energy in that it is a relatively invisible environmental impact of a product. Embodied waste is the waste generated during the manufacture of a product, or the manufacture of the raw materials of a product. As an example, take a yoghurt carton, before even including the yoghurt: paper is needed, generally waste off-cuts are rerouted into the manufacturing process so avoid being dumped, but effluents in the bleaching and dying process and the paper production process itself can be very polluting. The plastic used in the pot has another set of wastes associated with its manufacture, as do the aluminium foil cover that seals the pot, the cardboard tray on which the pots are packed and the shrink-wrap plastic used to hold the trays together. Every product we buy has a similar trail.

To try to calculate all hidden wastes involved in every purchase would be a daunting task. Yet to avoid making our purchases consciously would be to avoid taking responsibility for our environmental impacts.

Fortunately a very simple solution exists: the most straightforward ways to avoid hidden wastes are to buy local, grow your own and/or to minimise what you buy – and make your own yoghurt!

Keep in mind that beyond a surprisingly low level of material wealth, more 'stuff' does not buy more happiness. The basic requirements for living are essential to provide some degree of physical comfort, but above that level, happiness cannot necessarily be increased by boosting your income or your spending: i.e. by having more stuff.

Read on to the section on voluntary simplicity for pointers towards greater contentment without costing the earth.

Toxic and Hazardous Wastes

When we consider the term 'toxic waste', the images are usually of large polluting industries rather than the contents of the garden shed or the cupboard under the kitchen sink. Yet although toxic and hazardous wastes are generated in industry, they end up in our homes whenever we buy the products. The regulations for industry are more stringent, but some cover home use also. For example, many items are prohibited from disposal via the rubbish bin. These include what is termed *household hazardous waste*.

Household hazardous waste includes such items as paints, solvents, cleaning fluids, batteries, fluorescent tubes and CFLs, biocide containers, medicines and the like. They are many and varied, and have the potential for great environmental damage if disposed of inappropriately.

Traditionally such wastes would have been disposed of in landfill, despite the inadequacies of early landfill lining. Another route of easy entry into the groundwater is via the toilet. This is obviously an inappropriate way to get rid of paints, solvents, left-over biocides and other hazardous materials. Not only that, but your friendly septic tank bacteria won't stand a chance against such an onslaught, leading to poor treatment and odours.

Household hazardous waste is one of the components of landfill leachate that can greatly damage groundwater in the vicinity. Now most or all landfill sites and recycling centres have a designated household hazardous waste storage facility. Batteries have long been collected separately at landfill sites to stop the leakage of heavy metals into the environment as they decay. In most counties the county council- and industry-funded 'Chem Car' will travel around regularly to collect the following household hazardous wastes:

- Paints, varnishes, strippers and thinners
- Batteries
- Fluorescent tubes, energy-saving light bulbs (CFLs), thermometers
- Weed killers, insecticides, antifreeze, poisons, fungicides
- Aerosols
- Fertilisers
- Polishes, adhesives, glues, inks, sealants
- Cleaning agents, detergents, bleaches, disinfectants, caustic soda
- Waste oils
- Photographic waste (darkroom chemicals)
- Old medicines, waste cosmetics

Your local county council will be able to tell you when the Chem Car is next visiting your town for free collection of household hazardous wastes.

While appropriate collection is better than ad hoc disposal, the best option is elimination or minimisation at source. If it is possible to reduce ordinary household waste to a minimum, surely it is possible to eliminate (or greatly minimise) the toxic element within it. For example, if you choose to have battery-operated gadgets in the house at all, make sure that you try to use only rechargeable batteries. In this way the volume for disposal is greatly reduced. When buying electronic equipment ask about lead, mercury and other heavy metals content and potential for responsible recycling post use.

Instead of bleaches, abrasives, scouring agents and solvents (a.k.a. household cleaning chemicals) it is possible to get very good results with bread soda and vinegar. Personally I prefer to use natural cleaners on all kitchen surfaces rather than chemicals that shouldn't even be landfilled. For antibacterial agents a simple mix of tea-tree oil and water can be used for most applications. Lavender oil in the mix sweetens the smell and is itself antiseptic.

When it comes to waste minimisation, it makes a lot of sense to pay particular attention to items such as household hazardous waste. The lower the toxic element in our waste, the better. This is particularly true from an environmental perspective, because not only is the disposal of these items potentially hazardous, the manufacturing process is also more likely to be toxic to the local environment at the place of production.

Paints, glues and cosmetics are getting less toxic by the decade. Yet it is only by consumers diligently avoiding harmful products that manufacturers are inspired to source new ways to make the products we want. To hasten this change, carefully source the natural alternatives in your local health food shop and ask your existing retailer for natural alternatives to the conventional products. This sends a clear message back to the manufacturers and they will in turn change their methods to keep their customers.

The Potential for Zero Waste in Ireland

Is it possible to have a zero waste society in Ireland? In terms of the waste issue, Ireland is a very small country in a sea of production, consumption, travel, transport and transnational legislation. The potential is there, but should be viewed within the context of zero waste being an ideal to be achieved across our entire western culture (calling it a consumer culture would be an unfortunate place to start).

Becoming the change we want to see in the world is the only way to begin. Many countries around the globe have a zero waste plan, espoused either by their governments or by environmental groups in those countries, such as Zero Waste Alliance Ireland, listed in the appendices.

If we are to aim for zero waste, a multi-faceted approach will be needed, covering every sector of society from production to consumption. The different stages associated with waste generation, management and disposal are briefly described below, including:

- Manufacturing
- Retail
- Waste/Resource Management

- Legislative
- Societal
- Household

Manufacturing stage

Zero waste design – Design for reuse and easy repair, for recycling, for biodegradability. A big problem with reuse at present is that the design process for many products makes fixing things virtually impossible. With good design, the whole process becomes immediately more straightforward.

Keep the manufacturing process clean – eliminate toxic materials, substituting with safer examples where possible, e.g. some companies already substitute solvents with distilled water. Design for full separation of the component parts for ease of repair, reuse or recycling. Design for returnables and washables rather than for disposal. Returnables are clearly better than recyclables (e.g. washable milk bottles) because they use a lot less energy to get them to a usable state once again. Washables such as hankies, nappies etc. are more sustainable than the paper alternative, because whole forests do not need to be destroyed to produce them. You would be surprised how much havoc is wreaked in tropical and temperate forests just to get us our paper tissues!

Location – Minimise the distance your goods have to travel. Stay close to raw materials; close to the consumer; close to access for special parts – ports, airports etc. – and close to the recycling process. This spells smaller-scale production and the development of recycling industries within national borders rather than the present global market. A realistically high fuel price would facilitate this immediately. Even with the price hikes of recent years, cheap oil still makes the international transportation of waste and raw materials possible, but it is not a sustainable practice.

Retail stage

A good idea would be to introduce return facilities for reuse of certain items (e.g. printer cartridges are already collected by some companies and charities) and 'new for old' purchasing to ensure safe control of hazardous elements such as batteries.

Clear labelling is essential, including appropriate information such as product miles and embodied waste, as well as the existing recycling code. A waste labelling system like the current energy rating system for appliances would enable consumers to make a sustainable choice without needing a degree in environmental science.

A full range of recycled goods should be readily available and labelled as such. Repaired and reused goods would rate even better on the labelling scheme, because these would be effectively energy neutral.

Resource/Waste management stage

A careful charging structure is needed for the disposal of waste. This has already been introduced in many locations with pay-by-weight schemes, and the results have been almost immediate.

Good storage at recycling centres is essential to avoid deterioration of raw materials and saleable items. In some countries, unwanted consumer items are brought to recycling centres and put on shelves for resale rather than being dumped. This is easily carried out and can earn additional revenue for local councils.

Each recycling centre currently seems to have individual rules about what goes where for sorting. Full separation all the way through the waste handling process would presumably be more straightforward than mixing everything together and then exporting it for separation.

Ease of collection is a must. Ease of use and clarity of labelling at bring sites is essential to facilitate public use. The recycling centre locations are also important. Many small centres in the locations where people shop can be more user-friendly than one large facility with car access only. The latter is useful, but smaller bottle banks etc. are also needed to facilitate those without cars – a zero waste society built on motor transport does not really hold up in the sustainability stakes.

A good communication structure is needed between local councils and the public that they serve. Clarity is vital – even if that just means a notice board explaining what goes where at recycling centres. Explaining the 'why' is also useful, since it engages the public in the process and can help lead to greater care in sorting practise.

Public education is certainly necessary. Many people

still throw plastic into the fireplace, without any knowledge of the health or environmental implications. In fact, to move towards zero waste we will need education in all areas, from county councils to retailers, manufacturers and indeed everyone in society.

Legislative Stage

Tax adjustments are a necessary first step. The plastic bag levy is a good example of immediate public response to environmental tax measures. Taxes can help to balance in favour of recycled goods, for example to make recycled paper cheaper for the consumer, thus creating demand for the waste paper currently routed to the landfill sites. Taxes can also help tip the balance towards 'low waste' goods. Cellulose insulation, for example, is easier to dispose of than polystyrene and as such could be made cheaper to avoid landfill congestion. It also uses old newspapers, doubling the reductions of waste.

The challenge of charging fairly: pay-by-weight seems to be a relatively fair method of charging for waste collection. However, there have been reported problems since its introduction and the resultant rise in charges, such as a rise in illegal dumping and reports of people putting waste into neighbour's bins to reduce their own bin weight. These are more signs of a lack of public co-operation rather than a flawed charging system. Appropriate charging shouldn't be abandoned just because there are some who refuse to pay for the rubbish they produce.

Policing illegal dumping and the illegal burning of household rubbish is no easy task. Education and community action are probably the most effective ways to tackle the problem. If every known illegal dump was cleared and adopted as a local community wildlife area, with signs showing photos of the clean-up achievements, it would probably discourage most dumpers. Burning is more difficult to police. As long as incineration is favoured by some councils, it is difficult to convince people that burning at home is dangerous. Neither should be practised however, since they both contribute dioxins to the air we breathe.

Societal Stage

There are many different attitudes to the way we manage our waste, and a different incentive is needed for each. At the bottom of the scale are those who just don't care where or how waste is dumped. For them, legal enforcement is needed to prevent illegal dumping and burning.

Then there are the NIMBYs, who just don't want a new landfill in *their* area, but are happy to send their rubbish off as usual to 'somewhere else'. An example of this is a scene I remember from one of the towns protesting against a new landfill some years ago. Near the sign 'No Dump for Our Community' was a row of houses, each with its own wheelie bin waiting on the street for collection.

Then there is the approach that says, 'well, if the government/industry-employed scientists insist that incineration is safe, then surely it is safe'. Not so if you consult the scientists paid by the local environmental groups that try to keep the community healthy. It is difficult to get a balanced view from any single side in an argument, and science is often used to support an agenda rather than as a means to establish the truth.

There is also the group that asserts that everybody should be a self-sufficient smallholder. That is all well and good for those who choose it, but not an ideal lifestyle for everybody. Somewhere there is space for the realisation that there currently is a major national and global challenge to be faced, there is a solution and yes, while readily achievable with full cooperation all round, it *is* complex.

A national zero waste strategy has to be workable: many people will go to considerable lengths to pursue a more environmentally-friendly option, many more will not. The proposals need to function and need to be of some benefit to the user, whether that be a financial incentive, a legal obligation or a social pressure. As an example of social change, littering is no longer publicly acceptable, yet illegal burning of rubbish in the fireplace is still relatively common. As awareness rises, plastic burning will become as unacceptable as littering is now.

Household Stage

The household stage is the easiest, because it is the area within which we have direct control. For zero waste, maximise the separation of recyclables and reusables. Whether this is for recycling centres, recyclables collection, or for rerouting unwanted goods to charity shops and second-hand shops, it keeps the materials clean and keeps like with like for ease of handling and preserving maximum value for later use. Another zero waste household activity along the lines of separation is composting. Composting is essential, either in the garden, or as a municipal or group scheme for apartment dwellers.

The second prong beside separation of wastes is to make your purchases support the infrastructure that moves society in the right direction. For example, purchase what you can (of what you need) from charity shops, second-hand shops and the like. LETS, eBay, Freecycle.org, Buy and Sell and local free-ad papers are excellent resources from this perspective. For every new thing not bought, an old thing is not dumped. Direct reuse of materials saves on new purchases; cotton bags, glass bottles etc. can all be used over and over again. Indirect reuse can also be employed for many items, such as using old milk or yoghurt cartons as freezer containers.

A final, but fairly crucial element is minimisation of purchasing through simplification of needs and wants. A quick calculation of people and resources in the world allows us all enough for our needs, but not for our greed. Our western consumption habits fall into the greed category unfortunately, because we purchase well in excess of any genuine needs that we have, at the direct expense of others. Here's a new slogan: 'Shrink your bin for world peace!' Shrink your shopping basket might be more accurate actually, but the end result generally ends up the same. We can only expect world peace if we introduce equitable consumption and international trading practices. These practices start with us and our own lives.

Zero waste does not require zero consumption, but our overwhelming desire for new and bigger and more will need to become a little less extreme if zero waste and environmental sustainability are our goals.

Living More With Less – Voluntary Simplicity

Simplicity is an oft-repeated mantra in modern magazines and media. Unfortunately, the main point of its use in these terms still seems to be getting you to buy more products. But what is simplicity, and is it just a recent fad? How does it relate to waste minimisation and bin charges?

First let's look at what it is: my understanding of simplicity is that it is the practice of deriving more satisfaction from life whilst reducing the busy-ness of day-to-day living. That in itself is far from the advertisers' aim of selling ever more stuff.

Simplicity hasn't just jumped off the pages of household and fashion magazines within the last decade. Simplicity in one form or another has been actively pursued by those who value it since at least the time of the ancient

Greeks. Since then it has appeared in the writings of many cultures and traditions throughout the world.

Simplicity means different things to different people. A quick look at some book titles gives an indication of the ideas of the authors:

- *Voluntary Simplicity – Towards a way of life that is outwardly simple, inwardly rich* by Duane Elgin.
- *Living More With Less* by Doris Janzen Longacre.
- *Timeless Simplicity – Creative living in a consumer society* by John Lane.
- *Downshifting – practical advice on how to get out of the fast lane and find freedom* by Andy Bull.
- *Plain Living – a Quaker path to simplicity* by Catherine Whitmire.
- *The Simple Living Guide – a sourcebook for less stressful, more joyful living* by Janet Luhrs.

Many different factors may prompt someone to pursue simplicity in life. One person may want financial freedom from a mortgage and may downsize to achieve this. Another may want to have space and solitude for writing or painting. The spiritual and contemplative traditions have always held the concept dear. For some, the reason may be environmental consciousness or social justice, a wish to avoid using more than our due, or to avoid impacting negatively on far-off communities who make our cheap clothing and electronic equipment and grow much of our imported food. For others the motivation may be personal health or that of their family.

In these years, fashion is sometimes a reason for a sort of 'wannabe' simplicity, in which the latest Japanese blinds or Zen garden displace last season's something-or-other. According to Duane Elgin, author of *Voluntary Simplicity*, 'To live more simply means to live more purposefully and with a minimum of needless distraction'.

Typically a greater enjoyment from life is derived from such conscious living. More satisfaction then comes from what is already available, and there is less reliance upon constant expectation of possessing the latest advertised thing. Simplicity typically fosters greater self-reliance. There is also a greater sense of being able to choose your own priorities. If you do not take the official party line on how to live your life, you can begin asking yourself who you really want to be and what you really want to do. Advertising doesn't exactly foster such independent thought.

Consumption patterns vary hugely between today's world cultures. While 'simplicity' is increasingly used as an advertising tool, it is certainly not very visible in our aggressive consumer culture. This culture has led to consumption patterns that open a vast gulf between rich and poor nations, and the rich and poor in any one country. You are what you buy, it seems! But only if you play the game. As soon as you step outside the box, the magical lure of the advertised somehow begins to lose its grip and life can begin to replace the consumption addiction.

From a waste minimisation perspective, simplicity of lifestyle has a lot on its side. The less we buy the less we throw away. The smaller the house we live in, the less stuff we need to fill it up. What you may find is that health, environment and finances tend to go together. Contrary to what may be expected, the cheaper option and environmental option often go hand in hand, and are often healthier too. For example, if, instead of driving to the gym, you cycle to work, you burn less fossil fuel, spend less on the gym and on petrol and get more frequent and regular exercise into the bargain.

Energy consumption too has its solution in simplicity of lifestyle. The climate change issue is fuelled by our excessive use of electricity, oil and coal. Everything we buy has an energy input. Take house construction as an example. Timber has a considerably lower energy input than concrete and is thus better from a climate change perspective. Doubly so, in fact, because the timber takes up carbon during its growth in addition to being less energy intensive in processing than the manufacture of cement. Materials substitution is one thing, but simplicity steps in to ask: 'How much is enough? Why build so big?' The smaller the house the less energy used, regardless of the materials chosen.

At this point we could examine consumption patterns from around the world, but the point of simplicity isn't comparison, it is practice. Reduced consumption in poorer parts of the world is generally not a function of voluntary simplicity but is instead due to a lack of opportunity. Yet, if everyone in the world were to have the same consumer society as we do in Ireland, we would need about five planets to support the habit.

This isn't a guilt trip. The whole point of simplicity is conscious living; that you choose it yourself, rather than letting television, politicians or waste minimisation books tell you how to live your life. Simplicity offers a great deal towards our achievement of a zero waste, saner paced and more contented lifestyle.

Closing Words

The aim of this book is to encourage and assist you to get rid of your bin and in so doing to minimise your environmental impact. Having taken the time to read through these pages, take the time to try putting it into practice, at the pace that suits you.

Have fun with the process, and watch your savings grow to give yourself an added sense of satisfaction. When the book has served its useful function, pass it on, sell it or donate it to a charity shop, but don't let it hang around cluttering up your bookshelves taking up space …

APPENDIX I
SOURCES OF INFORMATION

Following is a list of information sources that I have found to be useful, not only in writing *Get Rid of Your Bin* but also in reducing my own rubbish output, as well as other sources that you may find useful. It includes mainly Irish examples, but extends further afield where appropriate. There are many, many more sources of excellent information on waste, the environment, composting, gardening and other related subjects that are not listed below. So do search further via your local library or the internet if you cannot find what you are looking for here.

Centre for Alternative Technology
Machynlleth, Powys, SY20 9AZ, UK
Tel: 00 44 1654 705950
www.cat.org.uk
'Europe's leading eco-centre'

Christchurch City Council
PO Box 237, Christchurch, New Zealand
Tel: 00 64 3 941-8999
www.ccc.govt.nz/waste/composting

Build your own recycled tyre worm composter. Also information on EM Bokashi and EM composting, worm farming and composting.

Construct Ireland
Temple Media Ltd,
Blackrock, PO Box 9688, County Dublin
Tel: 01 210 7513
info@constructireland.ie
www.constructireland.ie
Official magazine of ÉASCA, the Environmental and Sustainable Construction Association

County council recycling centres
All county councils have waste minimisation information on their websites as well as recycling information relevant to the county in question. Check the phone book for your county council numbers or search online to find the relevant website. There is a link to each county council on the Kildare County Council website at www.kildare.ie/countycouncil/links

Cultivate Living and Learning Centre
Essex St West, Temple Bar, Dublin 2
Tel: 01 674 5773
enquiries@cultivate.ie
www.cultivate.ie
'Cultivate's mission is to respond to energy vulnerability and climate change by providing access to the knowledge and tools to cultivate sustainable lifestyles and resilient communities.'

Enable Ireland

32F Rosemount Park Drive,

Rosemount Business Park, Ballycoolin Road, Dublin 11

Tel: 01 872 7155 or 1800 204 304

communications@enableireland.ie

www.enableireland.ie/contacts/shops.html

For the address of your nearest clothing bank call the above number or visit one of the shops listed on the website.

ENFO

17 St Andrews Street, Dublin

Tel: 1890-200191

www.enfo.ie

Ireland's government information service on environmental matters.

Environmental Protection Agency

Johnstown Castle Estate, Co. Wexford

Tel: 053-9160600 or 1890-335599

info@epa.ie

The website www.epa.ie/whatwedo/sustain/nwr/ gives links to the EPA National Waste Reports.

'The Environmental Protection Agency (EPA) has responsibilities for a wide range of licensing, enforcement, monitoring and assessment activities associated with environmental protection.'

Garden Organic

Garden Organic Ryton, Coventry,

Warwickshire, CV8 3LG, UK

Tel: 00 44 24 7630 3517

enquiry@gardenorganic.org.uk

www.gardenorganic.org.uk

'Garden Organic is the working name of HDRA (Henry Doubleday Research Association), the national charity for organic growing in the UK.'

Irish Country Markets

The Irish Food Market Traders Association,

Caroline Robinson (Chairperson),

Parkmore, Templemartin, Bandon, County Cork

Tel: 021 7330178

irelandmarkets@yahoo.com

www.irelandmarkets.com

Check the website for 'the definitive guide to producer and farmer's markets in Ireland.'

Irish Peatland Conservation Council

Comhairle Chaomhnaithe Phortaigh na hÉireann

Bog of Allen Nature Centre,

Lullymore, Rathangan,

County Kildare

Tel: 045 860133 / 860481

bogs@ipcc.ie

www.ipcc.ie

Excellent information on composting. Find out how to build your own worm bin at www.ipcc.ie/wormbin.html

Permaculture Magazine
Permanent Publications,
The Sustainability Centre, East Meon,
Hampshire, GU32 1HR, UK
info@permaculture-magazine.co.uk
www.permaculture-magazine.co.uk
'Solutions for Sustainable Living.'

PlanOrganic.com
Jim O'Connor, Hungry Hill,
Sandmount, Castletown Berehaven,
Beara Peninsula, County Cork
Tel: 027 70717
Info1@planorganic.com
www.planorganic.com
Lists products available in Ireland, where to buy – markets
around the country, and more.

Race Against Waste
Department of the Environment, Heritage and Local
Government, Custom House, Dublin 1
1890 202021 or 01 888 2000
department@environ.ie
www.raceagainstwaste.ie
Department waste reduction website and information.

Slow Food Ireland
info@slowfoodireland.com
www.slowfoodireland.com

'Slow Food aims are first and foremost to educate people about this wonderful culinary resource in the face of the over-commercialisation and homogenisation of our food.' Slow Food Ireland has local groups in Fingal, Dublin, Dun Laoghaire/Wicklow, Tipperary, South East, East Cork, West Cork, Kerry, Erne-Garavogue and Clare, with more groups being created.

Square Foot Gardening

info@squarefootgardening.com

www.squarefootgardening.com

US website of Square Foot Gardening originator and author Mel Bartholomew.

Sustainability Magazine

Corrig, Sandyhill, Westport, County Mayo

Tel: 098 26281

office@sustainability.ie

www.sustainability.ie

'The practical journal for green building, renewable energy, permaculture and sustainable communities.' Available in good health food shops.

Sustainable Ireland

www.sustainable.ie

'Ireland's internet portal to the world of sustainability, permaculture, ecological design, green building, renewable energy, and much more ...' Direct springboard to the websites of the Cultivate Centre, Powerdown Community, FEASTA, The Village, GM-Free Ireland, Sustainability and Stop Climate Chaos.

The Local Planet

Fivealley, Birr, Co. Offaly.

Tel: 057 9133985/9133962/9133119

www.localplanet.ie

'Ireland's journal on sustainable living.' Available in good health food shops.

The Simple Living Network

www.simpleliving.net

'Resources, tools, examples and contacts for conscious, simple, healthy and restorative living.'

Voice of Irish Concern for the Environment (VOICE)

9 Upper Mount Street, Dublin 2

Tel: 01 6425741

info@voiceireland.org

www.voiceireland.org

'VOICE of Irish Concern for the Environment (VOICE) is one of Ireland's leading independent environmental organisations, established following the closure of Greenpeace Ireland.'

Zero Waste Alliance Ireland

Ballybrado, Cahir, County Tipperary.

Tel: 052 42816

admin@zerowastealliance.ie

www.zerowastealliance.ie

Waste minimisation information. 'A policy and strategy for delivering real changes in waste management in Ireland.'

APPENDIX II
PRODUCTS AND SERVICES

Book Steps
4 High St., Bantry, County Cork
Tel: 027 52570
muriel@booksteps.ie
www.booksteps.ie
Holistic books and environmentally-friendly products.

Brown Envelope Seeds
Ardagh, Church Cross, Skibbereen, County Cork
Tel: 028 38184
madsmckeever@eircom.net
www.brownenvelopeseeds.com
Suppliers of Irish organic vegetable seeds. Excellent gardening information on their website – what to sow when, etc.

Buy and Sell
www.buyandsell.ie/index.php
Available in most newsagents, with extensive listings of second-hand items for sale, or wanted.

Compakta
Groundwork Leicester & Leicestershire, Parkfield, Western Park, Hinckley Road, Leicester, LE3 6HX, England
Tel: 00 44 116 2333566

mwaddington@gwll.org.uk

www.eco-coffin.co.uk

Cardboard coffins (your final chance to show off your environ-mental credentials!). Part of the Environ Charity of Leicester.

Eco Shop

Unit 1, Glen of the Downs Garden Centre, Glen of the Downs, County Wicklow

Tel: 01 2872914

contact@ecoshop.ie

www.ecoshop.ie

'Environmentally-aware shopping in Ireland.' Lots of products to help protect the environment. Excellent range of compost equipment to suit all your composting needs.

Ecobaby

56 Park West Enterprise Centre, Lavery Avenue, Dublin 12

Tel: 1850 525253 or 01 6205050

www.ecobaby.ie

'Ireland's leading suppliers of eco friendly baby products since 1995.'

Eco Natural

Tel: 01 4927774

info@econatural.ie

www.econatural.ie

Irish Eco Store with 'a wealth of natural, organic, eco-friendly and Fairtrade products for you, your family, your home and your workplace.'

Fruit Hill Farm
Bantry, County Cork
Tel: 027 50710
www.fruithillfarm.com
'Environment friendly house-, farm- and garden supplies.'

Gee-Up
Sitka, Blarney, Clogheenmilcon, County Cork
Tel: 021 4381485
geeupproducts@gmail.com
Suppliers of Gee-up composted horse manure for soil enrichment.

Greenfield Coffins
Chapel Road, Ridgewell, Essex, CO9 4RU, England
Tel: 00 44 1440 788 886
info@greenfieldcreations.co.uk
www.greenfieldcreations.co.uk
Suppliers of cardboard coffins and other cardboard creations.

Irish Association of Health Stores
Carrownalassan, Four Mile House,
County Roscommon
Tel: 090-6629981
www.irishhealthstores.com
Check the IAHS Members list to find your nearest health food shop.

Irish Seed Savers Association

Capparoe, Scariff, County Clare

Tel: 061 921866

info@irishseedsavers.ie

www.irishseedsavers.ie

'The ISSA is a voluntary organisation dedicated to the location and preservation of traditional varieties of fruit and vegetables.' ISSA supply seeds and seed potatoes to members, supply native Irish apple varieties and run courses and workshops.

Klee Paper

89 North Circular Road, Dublin 7

Tel: 01 8383544

www.ecoland.com

Eco-friendly stationery products and everything else for the environmentally friendly office, with links to articles and information answering the 'why?' of recycling.

Microbe Solutions

Jamesbrook, Midleton, County Cork

Tel: 021 4652429

tash@microbesolutionsireland.com

Suppliers of concentrated liquid EM and Bokashi composting systems.

The Baby Orchard

Brookdale, Upper Carraigadrohid,

Macroom, County Cork

Tel: 1890 252 265

contact@thebabyorchard.com

www.thebabyorchard.com

'Attractive, easy-to-use cloth nappies, and other beautiful natural products.'

The Freecycle.org Network

www.freecycle.org

'… a grassroots and entirely non-profit movement of people who are giving (and getting) stuff for free in their own towns. It's all about reuse and keeping good stuff out of landfills.' There are many Freecycle.org groups around Ireland, so check the website for details of the nearest one to you.

The Green Shopping Catalogue

Permanent Publications, The Sustainability Centre, East Meon, Hampshire, GU32 1HR, UK

info@green-shopping.co.uk

www.green-shopping.co.uk

'Ecological books, tools and eco-products chosen to help you live a greener, more environmentally-friendly, healthy and sustainable lifestyle.'

Walnut Books

50 Cornmarket Street, Cork

Tel: 021 4340348

www.walnutbooks.com

'Sustainability in a nutshell – environmental books.'

APPENDIX III
FURTHER READING

The following is a list of books which I have found to be helpful in minimising my waste generation and, in the case of the simplicity books, minimising my consumption. As with the other appendices, this list is indicative only of the vast range of material available on the subjects of simplicity, composting, gardening, waste minimisation and environment.

Breen Pierce, Linda, *Choosing Simplicity – real people finding peace and fulfilment in a complex world* (Gallagher Press, CA, USA, 2002)

Bull, Andy, *Downshifting – practical advice on how to get out of the fast lane and find freedom* (Thorsons, London, UK, 2008)

Callenbach, E., *Living Cheaply with Style – Live Better and Spend Less* (Ronin Publishing, CA, USA, 2000)

Elgin, Duane, *Voluntary Simplicity – towards a way of life that is outwardly simple, inwardly rich* (William Morrow and Company, NY, USA, 1993)

Fern, Ken, *Plants for a Future – Edible and useful plants for a healthier world* (Permanent Publications Hampshire, UK, 1993)

Hall, Keith, *The Green Building Bible (second edition) – essential information to help you make your home and buildings less harmful to the environment, the community and your family* (Green Building Press, Llandysul, UK, 2005)

Hart, Naoise Paul, *Green Pages – your guide to sustainable construction and development* (Sustainable Developments, Tuam, Co. Galway, Ireland, 2006)

Lane, John, *Timeless Simplicity – creative living in a consumer society* (Green Books, Devon, UK, 2001)

Larkom, Joy, *Grow your own vegetables* (Frances Lincoln Limited, London, UK, 2002)

Longacre, Doris Janzen, *Living More With Less* (Herald Press, PA, USA, 1980)

Luhrs, J., *The Simple Living Guide – a sourcebook for Less Stressful, More Joyful Living* (Broadway Books, NY, USA, 2007)

Ó Céirín K. and C., *Wild and Free – Cooking from Nature* (The O'Brien Press, Dublin, Ireland, 1978)

Pears, Pauline (editor-in-chief), *Henry Doubleday Research Association Encyclopaedia of Organic Gardening – the complete guide to natural and chemical-free gardening* (Dorling Kindersley, London, UK, 2001)

Philips, Roger, *Wild Food – a unique photographic guide to finding, cooking and eating wild plants, mushrooms and seaweed* (Pan Books, London, UK, 1993)

Ryan, Anne B., *Balancing your Life – a practical guide to work, time, money and happiness* (The Liffey Press, Dublin, Ireland, 2002)

Seymour, John, *The New Complete Book of Self-Sufficiency – the classic guide for realists and dreamers* (Dorling Kindersley, London, UK, 2003)

Seymour, John and Girardet, Herbert, *Blueprint for a Green Planet – How you can take practical action today to fight pollution* (Dorling Kindersley, London, UK, 1990)

Whitmire, Catherine, *Plain Living – a Quaker path to simplicity* (Sorin Books, IN, USA, 2001)

Whitefield, Patrick, *The Earth Care Manual – A Permaculture handbook for Britain and other temperate climates* (Permanent Publications, Hampshire, UK, 2004)

Woods, Caoimhín and Philips, Davie, *Sustainable Ireland's Source Book 2000 – Ireland's social, environmental and holistic directory* (United Spirit Publications, Dublin, Ireland, 1999)

INDEX

Contact Details:
FH Wetland Systems Ltd.,
Tel. 065-6797355
reeds@wetlandsystems.ie
www.wetlandsystems.ie